D1613997

Landmark

Study Skills Guide

JOAN SEDITA ◆

Landmark
Study Skills Guide

CHRISTINE DRAPER ◆

Master Notebook Chapter

JULIA W. HIGGINS ◆

Contributing Editor

Landmark Foundation

Prides Crossing, MA 01965

Proceeds from the sale of this publication are used to support
Landmark Foundation training programs.

Published by Landmark Foundation
Prides Crossing, MA 01965

Library of Congress Cataloging in Publication Data
Sedita, Joan
Landmark Study Skills Guide
LB1049.S44 1989 371.3′028′14—dc20 89-27870

ISBN 0-96241-190-6

Printed in U.S.A.
Text editing and page preparation by
Letter Perfect Business Services, Topsfield, MA 01983
Printed and bound by Wilkscraft, Beverly, MA 01915

Library of Congress Cataloging-in-Publication Data

Sedita, Joan, 1953–
    Landmark study skills guide / Joan Sedita; Christine Draper, master notebook
chapter; Julia W. Higgins, contributing editor.
    p.   cm.
    ISBN 0-9624119-0-6
    1. Study, Method of—Handbooks, manuals, etc.   I. Draper, Christine,
1954–   . II. Higgins, Julia W., 1958–   . III. Title.
LB1049.S44   1989
371.3′028′14—dc20   89–27870
                                                                                              CIP

◆ Acknowledgement and Dedication

In writing this book I have relied on the knowledge and experience of so many people that it is impossible to thank each individual. I gratefully acknowledge all the teachers, students, and parents of Landmark school with whom I was privileged to work over the years.

I owe particular thanks to the Landmark Outreach Program for sponsc ¸g this project. I would also like to thank my husband, Joe DelGuidice, and my parents for encouraging and supporting ɯe in the preparation of the manuscript.

This book is dedicated to my son, Marco Sedita DelGuidice, whose arrival coincided with the completion of this project. The joy he brings us is immeasurable.

◆ Table of Contents

◆ Preface

Landmark School is a program of the Landmark Foundation, which supports the education of dyslexic children and adolescents. In addition to the Massachusetts school, the Foundation also directs Landmark West, a day school in Los Angeles, and the Watermark program, an educational and sail-training program.

The curriculum of all the Landmark programs emphasizes the development of skills in reading, spelling, composition, math and study skills. In addition, attention is given to subject-area classes such as social studies and science, in order to build both general knowledge and study skills. This guide is based on Landmark School's extensive experience with study skills instruction in one-to-one tutorials, small study-skills classes, and content classes.

In addition to remedial education, Landmark School is involved in teacher training, diagnosis, and research. The Landmark Outreach program was founded in 1977 as the consulting branch of the Landmark Foundation. This program provides staff development and training, enabling classroom teachers to respond more effectively to the needs of students experiencing a variety of learning problems. Over the last several years, Landmark Outreach has received numerous requests for information on how to teach study skills. This guide is, in large measure, a response to the need represented by those requests.

The information in this book has been presented to thousands of teachers, and their reactions and suggestions were helpful in organizing the format for this guide. Although the Landmark Foundation is dedicatd to serving the needs of bright, high-potential dyslexic students, our approach to teaching study skills does not apply only to dyslexic students. For the many classroom teachers, special education teachers, parents and students who have asked for written material on Landmark School's approach to teaching study skills, we hope this guide will prove useful.

PART I

For the Teacher

◆Introduction

Reading, spelling, computation, and writing are considered the basic skills or tools for learning. Acquisition of these skills is emphasized in primary and elementary grades, and many schools expect that teachers will continue to teach these skills at more advanced levels as students progress through higher grades. Study skills are also basic tools for learning. Too often, however, they are not addressed in school curriculums.

The Landmark Study Skills Model

The term *study skills* means different things to different educators. Landmark defines it as a hierarchy of specific skills that build upon each other and help a student become an independent learner. This hierarchy includes organizational skills, recognizing and formulating main ideas, note-taking skills, summarizing skills, textbook skills, preparing for and taking tests, and research and report-writing skills. These skills can be taught in isolation (i.e., in a study-skills course, in a resource room, or in a study-skills center), or they can be taught within the program of a content classroom.

Why Teach Study Skills?

While it is not a panacea for every academic problem, study-skills instruction can improve the educational experience for both teachers and students. With study skills intact, students can reduce their reading time on long and difficult passages, strengthen their memories, prepare for tests, and be organized.

How do students acquire study skills? Some students have strong problem-solving abilities that enable them to develop study skills independently. For example, there are students who are never taught note-taking skills, yet they figure out a system for taking notes from lectures once they are in high school or college. Unfortunately, many students do not develop good study strategies by themselves and, therefore, cannot complete assignments successfully.

Most educators believe study skills are important, but too often, especially in the later grades, teachers place emphasis on teaching content and neglect to teach students how to learn. Teachers may assume that students were taught study skills in the previous grades when in fact they were not. Even students who have developed some study skills continue to need advanced instruction in these skills to prepare for the requirements of higher grades. When students enter junior high or high school, the academic demands on them increase in complexity. Consequently, basic study-skills instruction should begin when students are in the primary and elementary grades and continue throughout their schooling to assist them in adapting to more complex academic tasks.

Study-skills instruction teaches students how to be active learners and provides them with structured approaches to their classroom work and homework. These strategies help them avoid the anxieties created by the pressure to perform tasks that they do not know how to approach, such as taking notes from lectures or writing essays on tests. Even the best independent learners can benefit from study-skills instruction by fine-tuning the strategies they already have developed.

For Whom Is This Book Intended?

This book has been written for teachers encountering students who are unable to organize themselves and their work, read textbooks, take good notes, and study on a regular basis. It is also for teachers wishing to include more skills instruction within their existing curriculum. It is designed to be used as a guide, giving practical techniques and strategies for teaching, rather than as a textbook for students.

Classroom Teachers

A question asked by many classroom teachers is, "How do I find the time to teach study skills?"

This guide presents teaching strategies and examples geared towards helping teachers find opportunities in their daily lessons for teaching study skills. Some study-skills programs must be adopted on a grade- or school-wide basis, with student workbooks that require time out from the regular curriculum. By providing examples of how study skills can be incorporated into typical classroom situations, this guide shows teachers how to turn their everyday lessons into opportunities to show students how to apply study skills to learning content.

Teachers do not have to take a significant amount of time out from regular classroom instruction to teach study skills, although any time that is spent will actually save time by facilitating the learning of content material and creating more effective techniques for test preparation. For example, class time spent on textbook highlighting at the beginning of the year will produce better results with later textbook reading assignments. Likewise, a little time at the end of each class showing students how to write assignmments in an organized assignment pad may avoid a number of time-consuming confrontations with disorganized students who tend to confuse or lose homework. Classroom teachers will find that the information in this book can be incorporated into existing curriculum.

Skills Teachers

This guide will also be helpful to those who specifically teach study skills. Skills teachers have the luxury of skills instruction as a primary goal, and often an individualized teaching environment to accomplish this task. Resource room teachers, one-to-one or small-group tutorial teachers, and high school or college teachers who work in study centers or teach study courses will find this book most useful for its clear, sequenced approach to teaching each skill.

The more opportunities students have to learn study skills in as many classes as possible, the more success they will have in applying those skills. Teachers who teach study skills to students in an individual or small-group setting should communicate with classroom teachers about ways to apply study skills in the larger classroom. Students can better appreciate the benefit of using study skills when they see that it helps them learn in all their classes.

Parents and Students

The primary audience for this book is teachers, but Chapter 10, How to Be An Independent Learner, is included because of the many requests for study-skills information we receive from students and their parents. In this chapter, parents and students can review learning principles, as well as organizational, main-idea, note-taking, textbook, and test-preparation skills. Independent application of these skills by the student is emphasized.

How to Use the Landmark Study Skills Guide

Chapter 1, Teaching Principles, lays an important foundation for many of the teaching techniques presented in the skill chapters; there is frequent reference to these principles throughout the guide.

In Chapters 2 through 5, the skills of organizing, recognizing and formulating main ideas, note taking, and summarizing are presented as a continuum of skills. These basic skills are combined to address more complex, multistep tasks in Chapters 6 through 9 (textbook, master notebook, test taking, research and report-writing skills).

A Reference Book, Not a Textbook

This guide was written for teachers to use as a reference rather than as a textbook. Because students vary in their academic abilities and previous exposure to study skills, this guide is most effective if teachers adapt it to fit the particular needs of their students. The goal of this guide is to help teachers develop a way of thinking about study-skills that enables them to analyze a given teaching situation and determine how they can best incorporate study-skills instruction. The step-by-step progressions given for teaching each skill and the presentation of them as part of a continuum of skills provide a framework that readers can adapt to fit many different teaching situations.

Chapter 1 ◆Teaching Principles

Students have individual learning styles based on their particular combination of learning strengths and weaknesses, and teachers may find many types of learners in their classrooms. Some students learn best from information presented visually, others from information presented auditorily. How can teachers present information and give assignments in ways that suit the varied learning styles and needs of all students?

This chapter presents six teaching principles that help teachers address different learning needs at the same time. They are simple, common-sense principles, which many teachers already apply. The goal of this chapter is to help you apply these principles on a consistent basis.

Provide Opportunities for Success

There are some students in every class who, for one reason or another, have experienced some form of school failure. It may have been with their general course of study, with a particular subject area, such as math or English, or with a particular task, such as taking tests or writing compositions. This previous failure may create frustration, lack of self-confidence, and fear of certain assignments. These problems can be addressed by providing opportunites for successful learning.

When a new skill or lesson is introduced, provide easy examples and assignments so students are not immediately overwhelmed. When moving to more difficult assignments, intersperse easier problems with the more challenging ones so that students who are having difficulty can successfully complete at least part of the assignment. A little success can go a long way in encouraging students to keep trying.

Other ways to ensure success are to

◆ Make directions clear for class or home assignments to be sure students understand what is expected

- Have students write down all assignments and directions so they do not forget what is due or how to complete it

- Structure assignments so students who are having difficulty can approach the problem one step at a time

- When calling on students in class who are fearful of answering, ask questions that you know they will answer correctly

- Give immediate, positive feedback as tasks are completed

Use Multiple Modalities

Individual learning weaknesses may affect a student's ability to follow along in class or complete tasks to the best of his ability. Students with perceptual learning problems may have difficulty perceiving information presented visually or auditorily. Although their eyes and ears have picked up visual and auditory information accurately, there may be a problem with how that information is processed once it has been seen or heard. The information may be distorted, confused, or incomplete. Depending on how much information is given at once, or the speed at which it is presented, there may be gaps in what the student can process. Problems arise for some students when the learning weaknesses they have in these areas are strong enough to interfere significantly with their performance. Some may have difficulty in classes in which the teacher uses mostly lectures; others may have difficulty in classes in which information is presented visually through books, maps, and worksheets.

Materials can be adapted to accommodate different learning styles by using several modalities when teaching. Students should listen, write, copy, read, watch, reverbalize, and discuss what must be learned as often as possible. When presenting information, appeal to both the visual and auditory modes of learning. For example, when giving a lecture, hand out an outline of the major points or use the blackboard to give visual cues to go along with the lecture. A tactile-kinesthetic learning mode emphasizes learning through touch and movement. Teachers in the primary grades use this mode when they have students feel the concept of addition or subtraction by manipulating blocks.

Tracing the route on a map or copying visual information helps some students to remember it better than just seeing it or hearing it. Many teachers already incorporate several modalities when they teach; becoming more aware of this principle will help you to do this on a more consistent basis.

Micro-Unit and Structure Tasks

Micro-uniting means analyzing the parts of a task or assignment and teaching those parts one step at a time. Micro-uniting provides a blueprint for completing an assignment. This is one of the most useful of the teaching principles presented in this chapter, because it encourages teachers to help students who are having difficulty learning something by breaking it into smaller steps.

Just about any task can be micro-united. In today's high-tech society, people are faced with the task of learning how to use computers. Many feel it is an overwhelming, intimidating task, and there are those who would give up without even trying. However, when they are given a manual which provides step-by-step instructions beginning with how to turn on the machine, the formidable task becomes a series of manageable steps, each one building upon the other and leading to proficiency with the computer.

If students develop a micro-united approach to completing assignments, they too are not as likely to give up on tasks that appear confusing or overwhelming. For example, if, when assigned a thirty-page chapter to read, they receive this list of steps:

1. Skimming the chapter

2. Prereading the boldfaced headings

3. Developing reading questions

4. Reading one section at a time

they will be more willing and able to read and retain important information than if they read with no guidelines.

Providing structure is an essential part of micro-uniting. In order to micro-unit lessons and assignments, you must structure them so students can see the steps clearly and in order.

Insure Automatization Through Practice and Review

Automatization means learning something so thoroughly that it can be applied consistently and with little or no conscious attention. Sometimes students appear to understand something you have taught only to forget it a day, week, or month later. It is not until something has been learned at an automatic level that a student can count on remembering it and using it as a foundation for something new. Learning to drive a car is a good example of how automatization develops. When first learning, the driver must concentrate and think about every move. However, once driving has become automatic, the driver does not have to concentrate on braking or using turn signals, and is free to do other things, such as listening to the radio or conversing with a passenger.

Practice is the key to achieving automatization with study skills, and suggestions for ways to practice the application of these skills are given throughout this guide.

Teachers should take advantage of opportunities that arise to review previously learned skills. Showing the connection between current material and material learned last week or month will help ensure automatization for the long term. The skills in this guide build upon each other; this relationship should be pointed out to students. For example, the ability to recognize and formulate main ideas is essential for note taking, summarizing, and completing several textbook and test-taking skills. As you teach more advanced skills, be sure to review the basic skills.

Provide Models

One of the most effective ways to teach a new skill is to provide a model or example. When a teacher explains how to do something without giving an example, some students can picture what the teacher means and then try the assignment. However, many students need to see a sample of what the completed assignment should look like. These students use models as a springboard to begin an assignment. Using models does not mean that you are doing the assignment for students; it simply sets a standard to which they can compare their own work. In addition to being a catalyst for beginning a new task, models provide an opportunity for students to evaluate their work by comparing it with a well-done sample of the same assignment.

Note taking lends itself quite well to using models. For example, when introducing the two-column system (see Chapter 4), give students an example of two-column notes, along with the sample material from which they were taken, for comparison. After students take notes from a lecture, hand out copies of notes that you have taken from the same lecture so they can compare their notes to see if they have included all the important points. Taking notes on the blackboard as a class is another way to provide a model. When introducing highlighting skills, show students sample pages from their textbooks that you have highlighted. When assigning a composition or research paper, bring in examples of the completed assignment (perhaps copies of the same project from last year's students).

Include the Student in the Learning Process

As students enter junior high and high school, it is important that they become active participants in the learning process. They should develop an understanding of their learning styles, as well as why and how to apply study skills.

Teachers should include students when assessing progress by reviewing with them test results, written reports, educational plans, and comments to be shared with parents. Parents, teachers, specialists, and administrators determine learning needs and placements, but if this information is not shared with students, they will not be able to advocate for themselves as they grow older and more independent. The more students understand, the more confident they become as they devise personal strategies for learning. They will also be better able to communicate their learning needs to new teachers.

When students are aware of how they learn and why certain skills will benefit them, they are more likely to apply the skills they are learning when working independently.

Becoming aware of the purpose and rationale behind skills enables them to intelligently choose to use the skills. For example, if they can understand why using main-idea skills will help them comprehend a reading assignment, or why writing a summary and answers to study questions will help them remember the information and do better on essay tests, students will be more likely to apply these skills. When you take time to explain to students why you have designed an assignment or lesson a certain way, it is easier for students to take over the role of the teacher in deciding how best to approach that assignment.

Maintaining a dialogue with students on an individual and class level about the processes they are using in learning will increase initiative. This is obviously easier to do if you work with students one-on-one or in small groups, but it can also be done in a larger class. Talk through their process for completing an assignment by asking why they have chosen a particular answer and what they believe is wrong with alternative answers. Encourage discussion in class, and require students to go beyond simply giving the correct answer by having them explain why it is correct. Demonstrate the thought processes used in the application of a skill such as highlighting or note taking by using the blackboard or overhead projector to write out a sample based on suggestions from different students in the class. In short, use every opportunity to include students in the learning process so they can become more active, conscious learners.

Summary

These six teaching principles are referred to throughout the Landmark Study Skills Guide:

1. Provide opportunities for success

2. Use multiple modalities

3. Micro-unit and structure tasks

4. Insure automatization through practice and review

5. .Provide models

6. Include the student in the learning process

Application of these principles enhances your teaching style and ensures greater mastery of the study skills you teach. They are basic concepts that you may already use; the goal of this chapter is to have you consciously apply them on a consistent basis.

PART II
Basic Skills

Chapter 2 ◆ Organizational Skills

It is easy to assume that students, especially in the upper grades, have good organizational skills. Yet many students do not know what supplies they should bring to class, how to use an assignment pad, or how to determine how long it might take to complete an assignment. Surprising as it may seem, some students do not even know how to use a calendar.

Teaching Organizational Skills

Unless they are taught organizational skills, students will continue to approach their class work, homework, and test preparation in a haphazard and inefficient manner. The organizational skills in this chapter provide a micro-united plan of attack for school work, including organizing notebooks and materials, using assignment pads, using calendars and schedules, and organizing study space.

Organizing Notebooks and Materials

Show students that just as a plumber, carpenter, or accountant bring their tools to work, students must also bring their learning tools to school each day in a book bag or back pack. During the first week of school, give students a list of the materials they are expected to bring to class each day, such as notebooks, assignment pads, paper and pencils, dictionary, calendars, ruler, and calculator (example 2A). Send the list home to show parents what supplies might need to be purchased. Assign organization as homework so students take the requirements seriously. Keep a larger copy of the materials list on a bulletin board for the class to check each day to see that everyone has all the materials. For students who are especially forgetful, provide a daily checklist for their parents to review and sign until they consistently bring in the right supplies. With many students, you will be breaking long-standing habits and addressing some severe organizational weaknesses, so remember to be patient.

Present a standard system that all students are expected to follow for organizing notes, handouts, corrected quizzes, and homework assignments. Demonstrate how to organize this material in an appropriate notebook (see Chapter 7, The

Landmark Master Notebook System). If you tell students when and how to file information into these notebooks at the beginning of the year, and regularly reinforce their use, it will help students stay organized throughout the year.

Example 2A

Sample Materials Checklist

General Materials

☐ Notebook

☐ Pencil/Pen

☐ Paper

☐ Dictionary

☐ Calendar

☐ Assignment Pad

☐ Ruler

☐ Book Bag

☐ Other: _____

☐ Other: _____

Specific Materials

Science:	Social Studies:
Math:	English:
Other:	Other:

Color coding all the material from a particular unit is one technique for showing students in a concrete way how to group information into topics to study. For example, all the papers and notes from a particular chapter in a textbook might have a green check at the top of each page, with papers from the next chapter checked in blue. Another technique is to pair students and have them organize each other's notebooks and check to see if anything important is missing. Follow through by randomly checking notebooks.

Elementary school students are often intrigued by fancy pencils, notebooks or book bags. Take advantage of this curiosity by bringing in a large box of supplies and showing students how to put together a complete set of school materials.

On the other hand, a junior high or high school student may resist instruction in organization. For these students, begin by acknowledging the notebook system they have developed, then have them analyze how effective that system is. If a student can prove his system works, leave well enough alone. If changes are necessary, compromise with the student by allowing his notebook to be a combination of his and your ideas.

Organizing Assignments

Teachers frequently hear students say, "I didn't do the homework because I forgot what I was supposed to do," or, "That paper isn't due tomorrow, is it?" Tools made expressly for keeping people organized are available in stationery stores (pocket calendars, weekly planners, personalized lists of things to do). Many adults could not keep the demands of their jobs or family lives in order without them. Yet, who teaches us to organize what we have to do and when we have to do it? Requiring and checking assignment pads and showing students how to use them will create a significant improvement in the efficiency, timeliness, and quality of their work.

First, be sure students have good assignment pads. The common three-inch by five-inch pads are not very useful because they are so small. A larger pad that has sections for different subjects and room for other activities is much better. An alternative to having students bring in their own pads is to provide one that you have created and distributed (example 2B). During the first weeks of school, provide a time at the end of class when everyone writes down the details of homework assignments on these sheets. Include the purpose of the assignment, the due date, all the steps or guidelines for completing the assignment, and a rough estimate of how long it must be, or how much time it might take to complete.

Choose one area of the blackboard where you will write detailed homework assgnments so students can copy the assignments. Having the assignment written on the board and referring to it the next day will alleviate any confusion about whether you actually assigned something.

A response that teachers sometimes give to this suggestion is that it takes time they do not have. However, the time it takes to be sure assignments have been noted correctly often is made up by time saved not having to deal with assignments done incorrectly or not at all. It is tempting when you are running out of class time to call out an assignment as students are getting up to leave, but this makes it difficult for those students who have weak organization or direction-following abilities to be successful. Assign homework early in the class period and provide time for students to record it accurately and ask questions.

A note of caution about assigning homework: occasionally a teacher will assign homework that requires application of a new skill students may not be ready to apply independently. Be sure homework is related to the day's lesson, and assign work that students can complete independently. Even then, some students do not do homework, although they have written it down clearly and are capable of the work. If parents are supportive, work out a system by which they sign assignments when students complete them and you check for their signatures the next day.

Students often find it difficult to determine how long an assignment or several assignments will take to complete. They start their homework by taking out the first book they find and keep on working until they are too tired, their favorite T.V. show is on, or their parents tell them it is time to go to bed. They often stop before their work is completed and then scramble to finish homework the next day between classes or during lunch. Some students waste time because they do not

Example 2B

Assignment Sheet

Day _____ Date _____

Subject	Assignment	Time to Complete	
		Estimated	Actual

Long-Term Assignments:

Other Things to Do:

Today's Schedule:

8:00–9:00	4:00–5:00
9:00–10:00	5:00–6:00
10:00–11:00	6:00–7:00
11:00-12:00	7:00–8:00
12:00–1:00	8:00–9:00
1:00–2:00	9:00–10:00
2:00–3:00	10:00–11:00
3:00–4:00	

know where to begin or are overwhelmed by having several assignments at once. Homework is more manageable and less threatening if students learn to micro-unit their approach. Have students set goals for how much time they will spend on an assignment before they leave class. Then, ask them to note how much time it actually took to complete the assignment (example 2B includes space next to assignments for this). Show students how to make adjustments in their plans, and after several weeks of school they will have a sense of how much time to allot each subject.

You can also suggest that students organize their homework by planning the order in which they will complete subjects. Doing the more difficult assignments first, before they become tired, is usually the best approach. If students have a study hall or time during lunch that they can work the next day, show them how to pick one or two short assignments that they know they can complete in that time.

Example 2B has space at the bottom of the day's assignments for long-term assignments (such as research reports) and other things to do. Help students by assigning due dates to all of the steps in a long-term assignment. Make sure they write down these steps as part of their homework or they may forget and let all the work pile up until a few nights before it is due. Also encourage students to note any special tasks (such as stopping by the library to pick up a book) or personal commitments so they can make connections between school and personal time.

Organizing Time

Teaching students to use long-term calendars (semester or school year) and weekly calendars can improve their ability to plan study time, organize test dates, and plan special activities. With help, students of all ages and levels can learn to plan their daily and weekly activities. The more they are encouraged in class to use calendars, the more skilled they will become.

Start by placing a semester or school year calendar on a wall or bulletin board where it will be convenient to use during class time. Fill in all holidays, vacation days and other special activities on the class calendar, and always refer to it when discussing due dates or announcing a quiz or test. Mark dates so students can be easily reminded of upcoming events. By referring to a calendar on a consistent basis and talking about it as you use it, you help students develop an awareness of how time can be micro-united and planned. Pass out smaller copies of this master class calendar and require students to keep them in the front of their notebooks and to mark details as you do on the larger version.

Require students to keep personal weekly calendars. Many date books divide each day into time slots; students can use books such as these, or you can include a listing of time slots on the daily assignment sheets suggested earlier in this chapter (bottom portion of example 2B).

Comments such as, "I missed my meeting with the guidance counselor because I forgot when it was," will occur less frequently once students develop the habit of marking important events and referring to their calendars each day.

At the beginning of each week, share the goals for your lessons and announce any quizzes or tests. Have the students take out their calendars when you do this so you can be sure they are noting the information. If you have the opportunity to work individually with students, show them how to leave time for other things, such as sports or family obligations as they plan daily activities. Demonstrate how to set aside some weekend time to study for a test, use the library, or do weekly reviews.

Micro-uniting and planning strategies for completing tasks over longer periods of time are emphasized in Chapters 8 and 9 (Test Preparation and Test-Taking Skills, Research and Report Writing). Encourage students to use calendars at the beginning of the year, so they will find it easier throughout the year to plan steps for long-term assignments and coordinate their study time for several tests that might be given on the same day.

Organizing Study Space

Where students study and do homework is almost as important as how they study, especially for students who are easily distracted. If you have good rapport with parents and they are willing to set up a study space at home, describe in a note home or during parent conferences that a good study environment should include:

♦ A good light

♦ A comfortable yet supporting chair

♦ A clear working space free of visual distractions (such as posters or knickknacks) and auditory distractions (such as T.V., radio, conversations, or the sound of other children playing)

♦ A consistent place where the student always studies and, if possible, uses only for studying

♦ All necessary tools and supplies, such as pencil sharpener, ruler, paper, calculator, and dictionary

The setting of a finish time can be as important as establishing a regular time to begin homework. If a homework period is open ended, students may hurry their work. Setting a finish time encourages them to use the time to complete the work to the best of their ability. It also helps them realize that there will be time to do the things they enjoy after homework is completed. Depending on how long they are working, students should plan to take appropriate breaks to avoid becoming fatigued. They should complete one assignment at a time; all other work should be removed from the work surface so they do not become distracted or feel overwhelmed by the other assignments they have yet to complete.

Not all parents are able to help their children set up and maintain a good study place, and it sometimes frustrates teachers when they have no way to monitor what happens at home. At the very least, however, you can encourage students to think about setting up a good home space by practicing in the classroom. When students are working in class, require that they clear the desk of all material except for the assignment they are working on. Remove as many distractions as possible and take planned breaks. Model and discuss good work habits in class so students can emulate them at home.

Setting Clear Expectations

Students are better organized when they know exactly what is required in an assignment. When teachers are clear about their expectations for materials (notebooks, calendars, supplies, etc.), for classroom behavior, and for performance on specific tasks, students can plan accordingly.

It is important to share your plans for the week with students and to make sure they understand your expectations for homework before they leave the room. Be equally clear about your expectations for class behavior. Communicate with students the policy for requests such as being excused during class. When must they raise their hand and when is it all right to speak out? How do you handle missed homework or tests? Post a list of basic classroom rules for student reference and then stick to those rules.

Clarify expectations each time a new assignment is introduced. Some students do not know how long a writing assignment should be and may hand in too little or too much. Give examples and models, or tell them how much time they should spend on an assignment to do well. Before giving the first test, describe what the questions will be like. Will it be objective, essay, or both? How much time will they have? Can they use their books or notes? Be careful not to assume that students know what is expected. Encourage them to ask questions when they are not clear about what they should do. Call on students to reverbalize directions as a way of checking that they have listened and understood.

Summary

♦ Teach students to organize materials, assignments, study time, and study space to significantly improve academic performance.

♦ Help students independently apply organizational skills by explaining the rationale behind the skills.

♦ Model the use of organizational tools, such as calendars, assignment pads, and daily time sheets in class.

◆ Treat organizational skills as part of the regular curriculum.

◆ Clarify and communicate your expectations for the application of organizational strategies, and consistently check to see if students are meeting those expectations.

◆ Organize and clearly explain all assignments and classwork to avoid confusion about what is required of a successful student.

Chapter 3 ◆ Recognizing and Formulating Main Ideas

Recognizing and formulating main ideas are the foundation for most other study skills. When students learn to group information into main ideas, they have a tool that enables them to categorize, study, and express information in an organized way. These skills are like a key that unlocks the system for processing information. Students who are unable to recognize and formulate main ideas have difficulty retaining information from readings, organizing information in outline or note form, studying the appropriate information for tests, and researching and writing reports. They also rely heavily on details for responses and, therefore, cannot get to the point in a conversation or provide an adequate story summary.

Thinking in terms of main ideas is also a skill in everyday life. Give students examples of the many things around us that are grouped into main ideas. Food in the supermarket is located under the main ideas of dairy, meat, produce, etc. Books in the library are listed under main ideas of fiction, nonfiction, history, etc. When the evening news is reported, the announcer begins by stating the main idea. Just as ideas, places, and things around us are categorized by main ideas, information in school from lectures, books, and library research can also be categorized by main ideas.

A main idea can be the category for a list of items, the topic of a paragraph, the theme of an essay, the topic of a textbook chapter, or the thesis of a term paper. Main ideas can be distinguished from details, picked out as topic sentences, inferred, highlighted in a book, and paraphrased. Main-idea skills can be applied at a very basic categorizing level in the first or second grade; they can also be used to organize complex information from a college textbook. Main ideas can be found in oral and written sources. In lengthier material, such as textbooks, main ideas can be listed in a hierarchy consisting of major and secondary main ideas (see Skeleton Notes in Chapter 4).

Teach main ideas by following this three-step progression:

1. Categorize main ideas

2. Identify main ideas in paragraphs

3. Identify main ideas in multi-paragraph selections

Categorizing Main Ideas

The purpose of categorizing is to demonstrate that people, places, things and ideas can be grouped together into main ideas. Introduce categorizing by listing similar items and asking students what they have in common. For example:

♦ **Fruit** is the category (main idea) for apple, orange, banana

♦ **Emotions** is the category (main idea) for anger, love, sadness

For younger students and for students having difficulty understanding the concept, list related items and include the main category in the list; students then select this main idea from among the detail items. Elementary grade students enjoy creating lists. As they begin to understand the concept, they can create lists of their own. Two suggestions:

1. Have students list twelve flavors of ice cream, six holidays, five favorite books, or ten adjectives that begin with the letter "P."

2. Give students a list that has related items from two main idea categories and have them separate the items and label the categories.

Categorizing can also be practiced and reinforced in upper grades. There are many opportunities in content material for categorizing information. Some common examples:

Science:	Plant or animal species
	Types of weather
	Lists of elements
	Parts of the cell
Social Studies:	Names of famous people
	Countries or states
	Historical customs
	Details of historical events
English:	Parts of speech
	Sentence types
	Types of punctation
	Vocabulary
	Characters in literature
Math:	Arithmetic facts (multiplication, etc.)
	Types of measurement
	Algebraic formulas
	Types of word problems

As students practice categorizing content material, they will also be reinforcing long-term retention of the material.

Main Ideas in Paragraphs

The next step in the progression is to teach students how to recognize main ideas within paragraphs. When students learn to find main ideas at this level, they will be better able to understand, organize, and remember most written material. Even lengthy selections can be micro-united into paragraphs with main ideas and supporting details. Information from lectures and other oral sources can also be organized as spoken paragraphs with main ideas. Once students understand how main ideas and supporting details work together, their oral and written composition abilities will also improve.

Begin by using well-structured paragraphs that include a main-idea sentence and other detail sentences supporting that topic. Although the first sentence of a paragraph most often contains the topic, using some paragraphs in which the main-idea sentence is located in the middle or at the end will encourage students to refrain from assuming the first sentence always contains the main idea. Have students locate and then write out main ideas from paragraphs in class and for homework.

Another way to practice this skill is to use paragraphs containing a sentence that does not support the main idea. Students must read carefully and determine the main idea in order to find the sentence that does not belong. This will also prepare them to proofread their own paragraphs for unity.

Workbooks published by educational presses contain exercises for finding the main idea in which students are directed to select the main idea from a list of choices. When preparing students to apply main-idea skills to their content-area reading assignments, however, these materials are best used by having students formulate the main idea in their own words rather than pick an answer from several choices.

Next, teach students how to find the implied main idea of a paragraph that does not contain a topic sentence. The transition from identifying stated main ideas to formulating implied main ideas is difficult for many students, so be sure to provide plenty of practice with this skill.

Short, single-paragraph selections should be used initially. The one-paragraph news summaries found in most newspapers are a good resource for this material (example 3A). Remove the title and ask students to review the details to come up with their own main-idea title.

Paragraphs for practicing main-idea skills do not have to be specially prepared material. Paragraphs from the textbook, reference books or current-events papers that are already part of the curriculum can be used. When reviewing assigned reading, discuss the main ideas from key paragraphs. Ask students to formulate main ideas in their own words and put them on the board. Then elicit important details from students and ask how they support the main idea. Extracting the most difficult passages from an assigned reading and reviewing them for main ideas before students begin reading will get them started and improve their comprehension of the material.

Sample News Summaries

The titles for these news paragraphs state the main ideas in concise terms.

Heart Disease Still No. 1

Heart disease remains the nation's biggest killer, taking a life every 32 seconds, but researchers in Monterey, California have made "unbelievable" progress in taming the disease, according to the American Heart Association. Figures released Sunday show that deaths from heart and blood vessel disease have dropped 24 percent during the past decade. Researchers attribute the improvement to healthier living habits and better treatment.

Land Offer Nets Big Response

An offer in Minneapolis of free 40-acre parcels for people willing to settle in a remote county on the Canadian border has brought more than 4,000 inquiries, some from as far afield as West Germany and Guam. Homesteaders will be required to build a home and live there for at least 10 years. They are expected to be self-sufficient, so as not to drain the local economy.

Reprinted by Permission from the Associated Press

Main Ideas in Multiparagraph Selections

The final step in teaching main ideas is to show students how to recognize and formulate several main ideas from multiparagraph selections. Unfortunately, many writers, including textbook authors, do not always write paragraphs containing single, identifiable main ideas. Making the transition from recognizing main ideas in structured material to finding main ideas in common written sources may be quite difficult for some students. When determining main ideas in any type of material, analyze and discuss with students where the main ideas are and how they are developed by asking these questions:

♦ What is the topic?

◆ What is being said about the topic in each paragraph?

◆ What are the most important sentences?

◆ What do all the details have in common?

Begin teaching main ideas in multiparagraph selections using simple, structured material such as main-idea workbooks, student magazines, and encyclopedias. Have students determine main ideas paragraph by paragraph and write them in a list. Provide frequent practice so that students can automatize this skill. After they become adept at formulating main ideas from this type of material, move on to less structured writing, in which there is not necessarily one main idea per paragraph.

One technique for developing independent application of main-idea skills in multiparagraph material is the following:

1. The teacher creates a main-idea list based on a specific selection.

2. The students read the selection and review the teacher's main idea list.

3. The teacher discusses with the students which sentences in the selection contribute to the main ideas and which are supporting details.

4. The students determine where the information supporting one main idea ends and the next main idea begins.

Once this procedure has been practiced a few times, the following technique can be used:

1. The teacher distributes a partially completed main-idea list based on a selection.

2. The students determine the missing main ideas and fill them in.

Eventually, students can be weaned from prepared main-idea lists and create their own. Examples 3B and 3C include completed and partially completed main-idea lists from two reading selections.

Example 3B

The Christmas I'll Never Forget

by Richard Pritchett

On Christmas Eve for more than a quarter of a century now, John M. Horan, the postmaster in Stow, Massachusettes, has placed two refrigerator shelves beneath the family tree in the living room of his home.

They are ordinary shelves similar to those you will find in most refrigerators manufactured back in the forties and fifties. Yet Horan, who is 50, has preserved them carefully, guarded them from rust, and will always place them under the family tree on the great day.

On December 18, 1955, paratrooper Johnny Horan was a passenger aboard an Air Force C-45 high above the Cascade Mountains in the state of Washington. He had hitched Air Force rides to the West Coast for a reunion in Seattle with his Japanese bride, Teruko, who was arriving in the United States with their three children the next day.

Five minutes later, the trip became a nightmare. The wings of the small aircraft started to ice, and the C-45 began to tilt to one side. Then the pilot ordered all aboard to bail out.

"I went first," said Horan. "I already had my parachute on. I weighed about 160 pounds. Add to that the weight of the chute and the heavy winter clothes I was wearing, and I estimate 200 pounds left that plane when I leaped out. It was my 29th jump."

The others on the plane were not forced to jump. After Horan bailed out, the plane righted itself. Without the 200 pounds Horan had added to the weight, the C-45 was able to land safely at a nearby Air Force base.

"I landed waist deep in snow. I folded up my chute, tucked it under my arm, and started downhill. I figured eventually I'd hit a highway. Little did I realize how long it would take me to get down off that mountain."

Darkness came and Horan kept moving. He didn't have any matches. All the brush he passed was damp or buried under the heavy snow anyway, so it was impossible for him to start a fire. His only course of action was to keep heading down the mountain. When daybreak arrived he was still completely sur-rounded by snow.

Finally — it was about eleven o'clock in the morning, which was the time his wife and children were due to arrive in Seattle aboard a ship — up ahead, he saw a small cabin. The snow was still waist deep and the little cabin seemed an eternity away. It took him more than an hour to reach the shelter.

The cabin was empty. The only food available was a can of cocoa. But there was a wood stove, an old bed, and a refrigerator, but no electricity.

Horan found some wood in a corner and started a fire in the stove with some matches he had found on a shelf. Then he melted some snow and enjoyed a cup of cocoa, after which he hung up his soaking wet clothes to dry.

In Seattle his wife and youngsters were aware by then that he was lost somewhere on the mountain.

"I did the only thing I could do," said Teruko. "I prayed for my husband's safe return."

Three days later her prayers were still unanswered. A giant search had been conducted by the military and local authorities, but no trace of the paratrooper had been found.

Horan remained in the cabin for three days waiting for help to arrive. It never came.

"I was starving," he said. "The cocoa was gone, and I knew I'd have to do something if I wanted to survive. I decided to start walking again.

"To do that, I figured I'd need snowshoes, so I tore off some large shingles from the cabin, and tied them to my boots with some cord from my chute. I was off again — but not for long. I got about a half-mile when the shingles broke on me. It was back to the cabin again. I started looking around for something else to try as snowshoes. I spotted a refrigerator shelf on the floor. There was a second self inside the icebox. I tied a shelf onto each of my boots. They seemed comfortable enough, so I was off again.

"This time my makeshift snowshoes worked. Those shelves kept me up on top of the snow, and I was able to move right along.

"Still, I had a long way to go. Night came, but I couldn't afford to stop. I was hungry; I was freezing too.

"The next day I was still moving. By then there was less snow. Only up to my knees, I'd guess. Still, there was nothing in sight except snow. I was beginning to get discouraged.

"Then I heard voices. Two men were talking and laughing. They were somewhere up ahead — beyond the trees. I shouted again and again. They heard me and came running through the snow toward me. They knew who I was the minute they saw me. There had been quite a bit in the newspapers about me.

"Those men picked me up, snowshoes and all, and carried me to a place called the Rustic Inn, which is on the outskirts of a small town called Easton. I remember the first thing I had was a cup of tea. It was the most delicious tea I ever tasted.

**Example 3B
Continued**

"I remember talking to my wife on the phone. Then an ambulance came, and they took me away to the hospital. I remember, just as they were carrying me out on the stretcher, asking one of the men to give me those two refrigerator shelves. 'They are the best Christmas present I ever had,' I told him. 'They saved my life.'"

Reprinted by Permission From the 1984 Edition of The Old Farmer's Almanac

**Main Idea List from
"The Christmas I'll Never Forget"**

1. On the way to meet his wife and family, John Horan's plane ices over and tilts to one side.
2. Horan parachutes out of the plane which enables it to safely land.
3. Horan finds a cabin, lives on cocoa until it is gone.
4. He decides to walk, tries to make snowshoes.
5. Shingles fail, but refrigerator shelves work and he walks until he finds two men who rescue him.
6. Snowshoes from refrigerator shelves were the best Christmas present he ever received.

Example 3C

The Nightmare Life Without Fuel

by Isaac Asimov

Americans are so used to limitless energy supplies that they can hardly imagine what life might be like when the fuel really starts to run out. TIME asked Science Writer Isaac Asimov for his vision of an energy-poor society that might exist at the end of the 20th century. The following portrait, Asimov noted, "need not prove to be accurate. It is a picture of the worst, of waste continuing, of oil running out, of nothing in its place, of world population continuing to rise. But then, that could happen, couldn't it?"

So it's 1997, and it's raining, and you'll have to walk to work again. The subways are crowded, and any given train breaks down one morning out of five. The buses are gone, and on a day like today the bicycles slosh and slide. Besides, you have only a mile and a half to go, and you have boots, raincoat and rain hat. And it's not a very cold rain, so why not?

Lucky you have a job in demolition too. It's steady work. Slow and dirty, but steady. The fading structures of a decaying city are the great mineral mines and hardware shops of the nation. Break them down and re-use the parts. Coal is too difficult to dig up and transport to give us energy in the amounts we need, nuclear fission is judged to be too dangerous, the technical breakthrough toward nuclear fusion that we hoped for never took place, and solar batteries are too expensive to maintain on the earth's surface in sufficient quantity.

Anyone older than ten can remember automobiles. They dwindled. At first the price of gasoline climbed — way up. Finally only the well-to-do drove, and that was too clear an indication that they were filthy rich, so any automobile that dared show itself on a city street was overturned and burned. Rationing was introduced to "equalize sacrifice," but every three months the ration was reduced. The cars just vanished and became part of the metal resource.

There are many advantages, if you want to look for them. Our 1997 newspapers continually point them out. The air is cleaner and there seems to be fewer colds. Against most predictions, the crime rate has dropped. With the police car too expensive (and too easy a target), policemen are back on their beats. More important, the streets are full. Legs are king in the cities of 1997, and people walk everywhere far into the night. Even the parks are full, and there is mutual protection in crowds.

If the weather isn't too cold, people sit out front. If it is hot, the open air is the only airconditioning they get. And at least the street lights still burn. Indoors, electricity is scarce, and few people can afford to keep lights burning after supper.

As for winter — well, it is inconvenient to be cold, with most of what furnace fuel is allowed hoarded for the dawn; but sweaters are popular indoor wear and showers are not an everyday luxury. Lukewarm sponge baths will do, and if the air is not always very fragrant in the human vicinity, the automobile fumes are gone.

There is some consolation in the city that it is worse in the suburbs. The suburbs were born with the auto, lived with the auto, and are dying with the auto. One way out for the suburbanites is to form associations that assign turns to the procurement and distribution of food. Pushcarts creak from house to house along the posh suburban roads, and every bad snowstorm is a disaster. It isn't easy to hoard enough food to last till the roads are open. There is not much in the way of refrigeration except for the snowbanks, and then the dogs must be fought off.

What energy is left cannot be directed into personal comfort. The nation must survive until new energy sources are found, so it is the railroads and subways that are receiving major attention. The railroads must move the coal that is the immediate hope, and the subways can best move the people.

And then, of course, energy must be conserved for agriculture. The great car factories make trucks and farm machinery almost exclusively. We can huddle together when there is a lack of warmth, fan ourselves should there be no cooling breezes, sleep at such times as there is a lack of light — but nothing will for long ameliorate a lack of food. The American population isn't going up much any more, but the food supply must be kept high even though the prices and difficulty of distribution force each American to eat less. Food is needed for export so that we can pay for some trickle of oil and for other resources.

The rest of the world, of course, is not as lucky as we are. Some cynics say that it is the knowledge of this that helps keep America from dispair. They're starving out there, because earth's population has continued to go up. The population on earth is 5.5 billion, and outside the United States and Europe, not more than one in five has enough to eat at any given time.

All the statistics point to a rapidly declining rate of population increase, but that is coming about chiefly through a high infant mortality; the first and most helpless victims of starvation are babies, after their mothers have gone dry. A strong current of American opinion, as reflected in the newspapers (some of which still produce their daily eight pages of bad news), holds that it is just as well. It serves to reduce the population, doesn't it?

Others point out that it's more than just starvation. There are those who manage to survive on barely enough to keep the body working, and that proves to be not enough for the brain. It is estimated that there are now nearly 2 billion people in the world who are alive but who are permanently brain-damaged by undernutrition, and the number is growing year by year. It has already occurred to some that it would be "realistic" to wipe them out quietly and rid the earth of an encumbering menace. The American newspapers of 1997 do not report that this is actually being done anywhere, but some travelers bring back horror tales.

At least the armies are gone — no one can afford to keep those expensive, energy-gobbling monstrosities. Some soldiers in uniform and with rifles are present in almost every still-functioning nation, but only the United States and the Soviet Union can maintain a few tanks, planes and ships — which they dare not move for fear of biting into limited fuel reserves.

Energy continues to decline, and machines must be replaced by human muscle and beasts of burden. People are working longer hours and there is less leisure; but then, with electric lighting restricted, television for only three hours a night, movies three evenings a week, new books few and printed in

**Example 3C
Continued**

small editions, what is there to do with leisure? Work, sleep and eating are the great trinity of 1997, and only the first too are guaranteed.

Where will it end? It must end in a return to the days before 1800, to the days before fossil fuel powered a vast machine industry and technology. It must end in subsistence farming and in a world population reduced by starvation, disease and violence to less than a billion.

And what can we do to prevent all this now?

Now? Almost nothing.

If we had started 20 years ago, that might have been another matter. If we had only started 50 years ago, it would have been easy.

Reprinted by permission from TIME. *Copyright 1977 Time Inc. All rights reserved.*

Main Idea List from "The Nightmare Life Without Fuel"

This is a partial list of main ideas from the 15 paragraphs in Isaac Asimov's article. The student should fill in the missing main ideas.

Topic: Life in the future without fuel.

Main Ideas:

1. People usually have to walk to work.
2. Decaying buildings are recycled for natural resources.
3.
4. The advantages are that pollution and crime are down, and people are healthier because they have to walk more.
5. Electricity is scarce for lighting.
6. People wear warmer clothes and shower less in winter.
7.
8. Railroads and subways use most available energy.
9.
10. World population is high and many are starving.
11.
12. The lack of food has caused widespread brain damage in other countries.
13.
14. There is less leisure time as humans must replace machines to do work.
15. Eventually lifestyles will return to the way they were in the 18th century.

Students should practice formulating main ideas from a variety of sources so they can become proficient at applying the skill in all their classes. For example, science material is often presented differently than social studies material in textbooks. Also, use other sources, such as newspapers, reference material, primary sources, and magazines, which have writing styles different from textbooks.

Literary sources, such as short stories, plays, or chapters from a novel, provide good opportunities to strengthen main-idea skills. This material tends to contain less strucured paragraphs than nonfiction sources, as well as long passages of dialogue or descriptions of setting that do not contribute to the main idea. This unstructured material may also have several main ideas in a single paragraph. Students must carefully analyze each part of a literary source to determine how it contributes to the main idea.

Structure literary sources by narrowing the focus for recognizing main ideas. For example, have students list only the main action events or only the main ideas that have to do with a paricular character.

Additonal Teaching Strategies

The four suggestions that follow are for exercises that will reinforce main-idea skills in various classroom settings.

Suggestion 1: A Format Sheet

Give students the following reusable format sheet to help them follow the steps for recognizing the main idea in a paragraph:

Topic: (one or two words) _____

Main Idea: (in your own words) _____

_____

_____

Supporting Details (list in phrase form) _____

_____

_____

_____

Suggestion 2: A Student Sheet

Hand out the following sheet and have students refer to it when they are determining main ideas:

How to Find the Main Idea

1. To find stated main ideas:

   a. Answer these questions:

      ♦ Topic: What is the one subject the author is talking about throughout the paragraph?

      ♦ Main idea: What is the author saying about this topic?

      ♦ Details: Which details support the main idea?

   b. Find and underline the topic sentence that states this main idea.

2. To find implied main ideas:

   a. Ask the same question about the topic: What is the one subject the author is talking about?

   b. Use the details to determine what the author is saying about the topic.

   c. Create a topic sentence which all of the details support; this is the main idea.

3. Helpful Hints

   a. When looking for the topic of a paragraph, look for words that are most often repeated throughout the passage; they usually suggest the topic.

   b. Make sure all of the details refer to the topic sentence you have chosen or supplied.

c. Check your main idea by asking if it is too general or too specific.

Suggestion 3: Scrambled Sentences

Scramble the sentences from a short selection containing several structured paragraphs with topic sentences. Have students reorder the sentences into paragraphs so that main ideas are supported by appropriate detail sentences. Then have them create a title (the topic) for the selection. In addition to practicing main-idea skills, this type of exercise shows students how to arrange information when using research notes to write a paper.

Suggestion 4: Listening for Main Ideas

Present material orally and have students listen for the main ideas. If available, a television and video recorder can be used to have students listen for the main stories in a news broadcast. Using the stop and rewind features, a broadcast can be micro-united if the newscaster speaks too quickly.

Summary

A main idea may be:

◆ The category for a list of items

◆ The topic of a paragraph

◆ The theme of an essay

◆ The subject of a textbook chapter

Main ideas can be:

◆ Distinguished from details

◆ Selected as topic sentences

◆ Paraphrased in the student's words

Sometimes main ideas are stated in the passage, sometimes they must be inferred. Main-idea skills can be applied at a very basic categorizing level, as well as used to organize complex information.

Landmark uses the following three-step progression for teaching main-idea skills:

1. Categorizing main ideas

2. Identifying main ideas in paragraphs

3. Identifying main ideas in multiparagraph selections

When teaching main-idea skills, start at a level at which you know students can succeed. First, use simple, structured material; as the student learns the skill, introduce more complex material. Main-idea skills should be practiced using a variety of materials from different subject areas.

Chapter 4 ◆ Note-Taking Skills

Note taking is a procedure for recording information from lectures or readings in order to retrieve that information later and study it. When taking notes, students become active learners as they process information into their own words. Note taking is also a valuable tool for gathering and organizing pieces of research for a report.

Taking notes, especially from lectures, is a difficult task for many students. Teachers often hear students say, "I can't keep up with the teacher" or, "I can never understand my notes, so why study them." Given that note taking requires the integration of listening, interpreting, sequencing, and recording skills, it is easy to see why students may feel overwhelmed when they must take notes, and in some cases, why they develop a fear of the task.

It is important to teach students the value of taking and using notes on a consistent basis. Many students want to do the least school work in the shortest amount of time, yet still learn the material. They believe that as long as they understand a lecture or textbook chapter, their memory will serve them well, and taking notes is unnecessary. Until students see tangible success in the form of better test grades or higher quality papers, they may not be motivated to learn note-taking skills. Make taking notes mandatory and follow through by doing notebook checks in class. Help students develop the habit of automatically taking notes and copying information from the board by requiring them to take out their notebooks before class discussions. Assign note taking along with readings for homework and provide time in class for starting these notes.

Teaching Note Taking from Written Sources

Begin note-taking instruction by having students take notes from written sources only. With written material, they can go back over the information several times while taking notes. Build confidence about note taking by using manageable written sources before moving on to notes from lectures. Also, provide frequent practice at each stage of note-taking instruction to help students automatize the skill.

Two-Column Method

When students have learned how to recognize and formulate main ideas, they can use this skill to take notes that include main ideas as well as the accompanying details. Note taking should be introduced through the use of a two-column format. With this method, a line is drawn down each page of paper, leaving one third of the page on the left and two thirds on the right. Main ideas are noted in the left column and details in the right. Example 4A illustrates this format, and should be handed out to students when two-column notes are introduced.

Example 4A

Student Sheet:
How to Take Two-Column Notes

1/3 Page: Main Ideas and Submain Ideas	2/3 Page: Details

1. List all details on the right side of the page.
   — Use as few words as possible.
   — Use abbreviations.
   — Use markers to connect details and underline important information.
   — Skip lines as details change and leave extra space to add information later.
2. Write main ideas and submain ideas on the left side of the page.
3. Go over your notes at the end of class or as soon as possible. Fix up your notes and review the information.
4. Read through your notes in the evening and write study questions with answers.

The two-column method is the best way to introduce note taking because it is a concrete, visual way of emphasizing that information can be separated into main ideas and details. This format also promotes recording information neatly on the page. It builds on main-idea skills by requiring students to formulate and list main ideas in the left column, and then has them take one more step by adding the supporting details in the right column.

When you introduce this method to upper grade levels, students may claim they already have a way of taking notes and balk at having to use such a structured approach. Explain that this system micro-units information down to its smallest parts, and that once students automatize the skill of analyzing information in terms of main ideas, their note taking for longer, more complex material will improve. Linear note taking (outlining) makes it more difficult to see the information as separate main ideas with accompanying details; it appears instead as an overwhelming, steady stream of facts. Demonstrate to students that two-column note taking has an advantage over outlining because it leaves room to add or combine information from a textbook or later lecture. Students will eventually adapt any note system you teach them as they become more independent note takers, but using two-column notes at first will form good habits for future note taking.

From Lists to Multiparagraph Selections

The progression for teaching main-idea skills suggested in Chapter 3 should also be followed for teaching two-column note taking. Begin with structured, short selections and progress to more complex, lengthy material. Some of the same materials used to teach main-idea skills can be used to teach note taking so students see how these skills build on each other.

Introduce two-column notes by using lists that students have already worked with for categorizing skills. Students place the category topic (main idea) in the left column and the list of words (details) in the right. Some examples from Chapter 3:

Main Ideas	Details
Fruit	Apple
	Pear
	Orange
	Banana
Emotions	Anger
	Happiness
	Love

At the paragraph level, demonstrate how the stated or implied main idea should be written on the left side of the notes and supporting details from the other sentences in the paragraph should be written on the right (example 4B).

Students can then take notes from multiparagraph material. Structured material with one main idea per paragraph should have the same number of main ideas in the left column of notes as the number of paragraphs. Example 4C illustrates how a structured, four-paragraph article can be grouped into main ideas and details.

Less Structured Material

Once students have learned to apply two-column note-taking skills using structured material, less structured material should be introduced. A variety of written sources can be used for practice, including newspapers, magazine articles, encyclopedia entries, and textbooks.

Some students tend to write everything down and may have difficulty determining which information is irrelevant. On the other hand, students who write down just a few notes may have difficulty including everything important. One way that students can test their notes to see if they are complete is for the teacher to give an open-notes quiz. Students must use their notes during the quiz to find answers; credit is given for a correct answer only when it can be underlined in the notes. This exercise underscores the importance of taking thorough notes. After the quiz, ask students whether each quiz question dealt more with a main concept (left-column notes) or with a fact, example or definition (right-column notes). This will help emphasize the usefulness of studying information in terms of main ideas and details.

Example 4B

Behavior of Groups

There are many reasons why people affiliate, or join, with others in groups. We are members of a family group by birth or adoption. We join clubs because we like to sing, ski, hike, or participate in some other activity a group offers. If you go to a crowded football game, you have a kind of fun you could not have by yourself. People tend to join groups when danger threatens, because in associating with others they feel more secure. Also, it is only by joining with others and working together that people can achieve certain goals, such as persuading their senator to support a certain bill or raising money for their senior class.

Taken from the textbook Invitation to Psychology *by Ragland and Saxon, page 401. Reprinted by permission from Scott, Foresman and Company. Copyright 1985.*

Main Idea	Details
Reasons why people group together	Born or adopted into a family group
	To participate in group activity
	Can have more fun in groups
	Can feel more secure in a group
	To get help in achieving goals

Provide models of two-column notes so students can see what their notes should look like. Distribute a copy of sample two-column notes with reading selections, then explain how information was pulled from the paragraphs and into the two columns. Assign a similar selection for homework, and the next day, hand out a copy of your notes again so students can compare and analyze their work. Pair students up and have them exchange notes to determine if

Example 4C

Juvenile Juries — Peer Pressure at Work

On the theory that it takes a teen-ager to know a teen-ager, juvenile juries in Denver are deciding the sentences given to some first-time offenders at the junior and senior high school level. The student jurors, volunteers all, pass sentence only on young people who have admitted guilt and signed contracts with the district attorney's office agreeing to abide by whatever penalty their peers impose. The juries handle such crimes as assault, possession of dangerous weapons or marijuana—all but the most serious. Typical sentences include unpaid community service, obeying tight curfews, avoiding the city's high-crime Capitol Hill area, attending school, getting a job or making full restitution in cases of theft or vandalism.

Given the choice, virtually all delinquents opt for sentencing by the youthful juries. "It's a lot better than going before a judge," says a 16 year old who stole a car at knife point and was required to accept counseling and strict curfew rules for a year. "It was good to talk to someone who understands," he says of his jury.

The volunteer juries have turned out to be sensitive and imaginative. They have handed out some less-than-draconian but effective decrees: ordering a 17 year old to join an athletic team; rebuking a father for belittling his son and "being part of the problem"; instructing a youth to write a letter of apology to a policeman. Says Zoralee Steinberg, who heads Denver County's "diversion" (i.e., from the criminal justice system) program for young offenders: "The insight these kids have is amazing."

Denver County District Attorney, Dale Tooley, who with Steinberg presented the jury program to the students last spring, believes one reason for its success is that the kids get a hearing within days after their arrest, instead of brooding for two or three months while awaiting conventional trial. More important perhaps is the program's philosophy that young people are responsible for their actions, coupled with close follow-up; the district attorney's office remembers delinquents on holidays and birthdays—even after they have left the program—makes sure that they observe whatever curfew is set. So far, only one of the 55 offenders sentenced by juvenile juries has been charged with another crime.

Two-Column Notes from "Juvenile Juries"

Main Ideas	Details
juvenile offenders sentenced by juvenile juries in Denver	— student jurors volunteer — only sentence offenders who admit guilt and sign contract with district attorney accepting penalty — sentences — community service, strict curfews, school attendance, job, pay back for theft
juvenile jurors popular	— better than judge, more understanding
juries give sensitive, imaginative, and effective judgment	— join athletic team — letter of apology
reasons for jury program success	— hearing soon after arrest — believe young people responsible for actions — good follow-up remembering birthdays and holidays — only 1 in 55 sentenced twice

important information was left out or if irrelevant information should be removed. Another strategy for helping students apply this skill independently is to hand out a partially filled note sheet and have students fill in the missing main ideas and details.

Encourage class discussion about notes. Plan a lesson in which you take notes on the board based on student suggestions. Ask different students if these notes are complete. Once students get used to working as a group, they will not hesitate to disagee with one another, and working as a class provides a good opportunity to show students how notes can be fine-tuned.

Subskills

There are three subskills that students must learn to be good note takers:

1. Abbreviating

2. Employing word economy

3. Using visual markers to organize notes

It is frequently assumed that students, especially by the time they reach high school, have learned these basic skills. However, many students need specific instruction in these areas. It is hard to believe that a sixteen year old would not know that "Mr." is an abbreviation for "Mister," or "vs." for "versus," but if you ask students to abbreviate a list of common words, you may be surprised to see how many lack this skill.

Commonly accepted abbreviations like the two examples above, as well as symbols such as "w/" for "with" and " + " for "and" should be reviewed. Encourage students to use the first syllable or part of a word instead of writing full words out (e.g., "cap" for "capital" or "subj" for "subject"). Omitting vowels from some words is also a good way to abbreviate (e.g., "prps" for "purpose"). Pass out a list of common abbreviations and require that students refer to the list during note-taking lessons. When modeling notes on the board, point out ways that certain terms that come up regularly in the material can be abbreviated. Exercises to develop and practice abbreviation skills can be fun and do not require much time. Give students lists of words to abbreviate or give them lists of abbreviations that they must turn back into words. Divide the class into teams and have contests with abbreviation exercises. Learning how to use abbreviations automatically will save time and writing energy, especially when taking notes from lectures.

Word economy is just as important as abbreviating. Many students copy whole sentences from their readings or try to write every word from a lecture. One way to practice writing notes with a minimum of words is to telegraph sentences. Students are charged points for every letter and word they use to translate a sentence into a telegraph note. Students compete to see who has the fewest points from notes that are still readily understood by class members. Another technique is to pass out samples of notes you have taken that are too wordy, and then have students make the notes more concise. When reviewing student notes, point out or draw lines through words and phrases that are not necessary. Students can exchange notes and check each others' work for economy of words.

Finally, show students how to use visual markers to better organize notes on the page. Some suggestions:

♦ Lines should be drawn across the page to separate topics and main ideas.

♦ Colored markers should be used to highlight important information.

♦ Details or definitions should be numbered and key words underlined.

♦ Space should be left after each main idea so information can be added later.

Teaching Note Taking from Lectures and Nonwritten Sources

When taking notes from a written source, students can go back over the material to be sure they have all the important information, and they can read and write notes at their own pace. However, taking notes from a lecture, class discussion, movie, filmstrip, or other nonwritten source is more difficult because the student cannot control the rate at which the material is presented or take time to review the material.

Given the difficulty of the task and the fact that some students have developed an aversion to taking notes, it is particularly important to use structured assignments that are geared for success. Teach the skill one step at a time and provide a lot of practice until students feel confident about their ability to take notes from oral sources.

Teachers sometimes think that skills for taking notes from lectures are not needed until high school because elementary teachers do not give formal lectures. However, a simple task such as listening and writing down directions for homework in an assignment book is a form of note taking that is used in elementary grades. Audio-visual aids are frequently used in fourth through eighth grade content classes, and students are expected to remember the information from educational movies and filmstrips for tests. When a teacher in a junior high class asks that notes be taken, it is not unusual to see some of the students trying to write everything down, while many of the others are scribbling just a few words. When instruction in good listening and note-taking skills begins in the early grades, students gradually develop the ability to take notes from more advanced oral presentations in later grades.

Two-Column Note Taking from Lectures

Once students have been taught the two-column format with practice from written sources, introduce note taking from oral sources using the same system. Students should listen for main ideas and group information into supporting details from spoken information just as they did from written information. During a lesson presented orally, take the time to write the main ideas you are presenting on the left side of the board and details on the right. A list of the main ideas may also be put on the board before the talk begins; as details are given, they are added. Emphasize the division of main ideas from details in oral presentations by handing out a two-column sheet of notes and ask students to follow as you present. As students develop note-taking skills, provide partially filled-in notes from a lecture for them to complete during the presentation. Eventually, provide only a skeleton page with blank spaces where the main ideas and details are to be added.

Material for introducing and developing this skill should follow the same progression suggested for teaching main ideas and note taking from written sources. Begin by conducting a short, preplanned oral presentation that has one clear main idea and a few details. Limit what students listen for by presenting the information orally three times. The first time, students should listen without taking notes. The second time they should identify the main idea and write it down, and the third time they should listen for the details and write them down. Depending on student abilities, you might have to micro-unit this task even further by telling the students how many details there will be.

Next, give an oral presentation that closely follows a structured, multiparagraph selection with several main ideas. Repeat the presentation several times so students can take notes on main ideas and then details. Provide enough practice with this type of material so that students feel confident about note taking at this level. As presentations become more complex, show students how to leave spaces in their notes for questions marks if they feel they have missed something; they should be encouraged to ask the teacher or a fellow classmate for this information after the lecture. Teach students to continue writing details in the right column even if they are not sure what the main idea is. Main ideas sometimes have to be formulated and added in the left column later, especially if the speaker does not state the main point at the beginning of the presentation.

Once students become adept at listening for main ideas and details, teachers can base their presentations on more difficult and varied material for note-taking practice. A presentation can be recorded on a tape machine and segments of the talk reviewed by using the pause and reverse controls of the recorder. This type of exercise provides time for class discussion about how notes should be taken. Use a videotaped recording of a newscast or other informational program that can be stopped and played back to discuss application of note-taking skills. When you are lecturing, stop to ask, "What was the main idea of what I said?" or, "How many details did I just give to support my point?" Taking this time to talk about how notes are taken and to follow through by checking student notes on a frequent basis, will promote independent application of note-taking skills.

Notes from an Interview

Note taking from oral sources can also be introduced by having students take notes from an interview. The advantage of using an interview as a source is that the student can determine the questions (main ideas) ahead of time. They can also exercise some control over the pace of the oral responses by finishing their notes on one question before asking another. Students can interview each other, parents, friends, or teachers. Example 4D includes questions for an interview about someone's family. The questions are written in the left column as main ideas, and the answers will become the details in the right column.

Example 4D

Note Taking from an Interview

Main Idea Questions	Detail Answers
What are the names and ages of the people in your family?	
Can you give a job or hobby that each family member has?	
Where does your family live? Have they ever lived somewhere else?	
Can you tell me three in-teresting things about your family?	

Students can also be assigned to take notes from a scene. They choose a place where they can take notes on what is going on (such as lunch in the cafeteria or study hall in the library). Main idea questions (e.g., Who is in the room? What are they doing?) are written ahead of time in the left column, and the detail notes are taken in the right.

Subskills for Lecture Notes

An important subskill for note taking from lectures is recognizing cues from the speaker that will aid note taking. Review with students the following cues:

1. A speaker usually pauses before moving on to another idea.

2. When something is repeated or emphasized, it usually is important and should be highlighted in the notes.

3. Transition words such as "next," "finally," "the most important . . .," etc., signal important information.

4. A speaker can give subtle organizational clues through body language (shifting weight, looking back at notes, etc.).

5. Introductory and concluding remarks often provide a good summary of the main ideas in the presentation.

Take a moment during your own lectures and class discussions to point out examples of cues you have used. Many students are not aware of these simple but helpful tips.

Editing notes after they have been taken is another subskill that should be taught. To revise notes so that they are in the best form for studying, students must first be sure that all the main ideas have been included and that the accompanying details clearly support these main ideas. Notes should always be reviewed soon after they are taken to determine if information was missed so students can ask questions and fill in missing material.

Example 4E lists steps to follow when taking notes from a lecture. It should be given to students and reviewed whenever they are going to take notes from a lecture.

Selective Note Taking

When students take notes from sources for a paper or special project such as a debate, they must apply selective note-taking skills. In taking notes from lectures or reading assignments, all important information is noted. When doing research, students must sort through a large body of information and select only information that pertains to their topic.

Selective note-taking skills are used at elementary through college levels. A fourth-grade student who is preparing a one-page report about beagles applies selective note taking as he reads an encyclopedia entry about dogs. A high school senior uses selective note taking to gather evidence from several news articles to support a debate position. Teachers should not take for granted that students will develop successful selective note-taking strategies on their own; it can and should be taught.

Example 4E

Student Sheet:
How to Listen and Take Notes from a Lecture

1. Anticipate what the lecturer will discuss
   - review notes from the previous lecture
   - complete related readings before you come to class
   - refer to any handouts the teacher gives before or during the lecture

2. Use the two-column format and take organized notes
   - listen for main ideas by asking "What is the point of this?"
   - listen for details by asking "Is this information relevant and does it support a main idea?"
   - abbreviate and use simple phrasing
   - use lines and other visual markers to separate, emphasize and organize notes

3. Look for cues from the speaker
   - notice body language (shifts in position, pauses, etc.)
   - listen for signal and transition words such as
     "the next..."
     "first...second...final"
     "there are four reasons..."
   - be sure to note remarks that are repeated or emphasized

4. Be an active listener
   - sit close to the speaker so you can see and hear better
   - leave room in your notes for information you missed and ask clarifying questions during or after the lecture

---

Introduce selective note taking by choosing a structured reading selection about an issue that has two sides to it, such as the pros and cons of children watching television. Have students read the selection and underline the sentences that support one side of the issue (i.e., watching television is helpful). Have students write this information into two- column notes. Next, have the students search for statements to support the opposing position (i.e., the negative aspects of children watching television). Later, you can have students use the notes from this exercise to stage a class debate.

Another assignment for developing selective note-taking skills is to use an encyclopedia entry about a major city. Choose a subtopic, such as the history of the city, and have students search for information that pertains just to this subtopic. There may be a specific section in the entry just for history; this is where students will find most of the information on this subtopic. However, information may also be found about the history of the city in other, less obvious sections of the entry. Encourage students to read the entire encyclopedia entry carefully to search for appropriate information. Do the first city as a class assignment by reading sections together and asking the class if material should be noted or not. Then assign another city for students to take notes on by themselves. Eventually, students can use their notes to write a composition about the history of one of these cities.

When students can take notes on a specific topic from one source, progress to having them take notes on a topic from several sources. For example, a sixth grade teacher can give students material from the following sources about lobsters:

♦ A dictionary entry

♦ A short encyclopedia entry

♦ A paragraph from a cookbook on lobsters

♦ A section from an article about lobstermen

Choose a subtopic, such a physical description of lobsters or how humans use lobsters. Have students read the sources and underline only the information that pertains to that subtopic. Underlined sentences should be reduced to note phrases and organized into main ideas and supporting details on the note page. Some sources will contain a lot of information that should go in the notes, while others may contain very little.

This assignment can be made more challenging for older, advanced students by using more difficult material. Choose a famous American and collect information about that person from a major encyclopedia, a book of facts and dates, an annotated biography, a general American history book, and another source such as a political or art history book. Assign several subtopics about this person to individuals or teams of students. Have them selectively take notes on topics such as family life, childhood, specific accomplishments, or monuments dedicated to the person's achievements. Take the students through the process step by step and have them explain why they have included each piece of data. Later, the notes can be used to write a report about the famous individual.

Skeleton Notes of Main Ideas

Although the two-column method is an excellent approach for introducing note taking and works well with short selections, students need a different approach for noting layers of main ideas in lengthier material such as a textbook. Taking two-column notes paragraph by paragraph from a twenty-page chapter is cumbersome and time consuming. By forming a skeleton outline of main ideas, students can quickly create an overview of the main points and how they relate to each other. To create a skeleton outline, students apply advanced main-idea skills to determine the hierarchy of main ideas. As they read, they should ask the following questions:

♦ What is the main topic of the chapter?

♦ How many sections (main categories of information) is the chapter broken into?

♦ How many main ideas make up each section?

♦ What specific main ideas are presented in the paragraphs?

Most textbooks use larger, bold print for titles of chapters, major sections, and main points within these sections. Have students use these headings to help determine main ideas. They should form a list of main ideas that visually organizes how the major, minor and paragraph ideas are related by using an outlining format (as example 4F illustrates).

Example 4F

Sample Skeleton Outline

First section in chapter _____

    Main point_____

        Sub-main ideas (from paragraphs) _____

        _____

        _____

        _____

        _____

    Main point_____

        Sub-main ideas (from paragraphs) _____

        _____

        _____

        _____

        _____

Second section in chapter _____

    Main point_____

        Sub-main ideas (from paragraphs) _____

        _____

        _____

        _____

        _____

By preparing a skeleton outline, the student establishes categories for organizing information as he reads the textbook. A similar list of main ideas can be created from a week's worth of lecture notes or from combinations of main ideas from several sources used in class. These overview notes of main concepts provide a structured, micro-united approach for reviewing information and studying for a test.

Additional Teaching Strategies

The five suggestions that follow are for exercises that will reinforce note-taking skills.

Suggestion 1: Prepare Prelecture Questions

Hand out questions before giving a lecture or assigning a reading. Divide the questions into those that have main ideas as answers and those that have details as answers. Have students review the questions and tell them to listen or read for the answers. This assignment will reinforce listening and reading with a purpose, as well as help students group information for notes into main ideas and details.

Suggestion 2: Assign Oral Presentations

Have students prepare and give brief oral presentations to the class. The topics can be something of personal interest, such as "show and tell" talks, or more formal presentations of material from the textbook or other reference sources. Encourage presenters to organize their material by main ideas and details so other students can take notes. While each student presents, take two-column notes on the board as a model. In addition to providing an opportunity to model note-taking skills, this technique also helps students become used to different presentation styles and rates of speaking.

A similar strategy is to have students use the notes they take from the teacher's lecture to retell that lecture the next day or later in the week.

Suggestion 3: Review Main Ideas

Write main ideas on the board before or while you lecture. Keep the notes there until the next day. Begin the next day's lesson by pointing to each main idea and asking students to review information that was presented the day before. Encourage them to use their notes to answer instead of relying just on memory. Remind them to add anything from this review that might be missing from their notes.

Suggestion 4: Prioritize Notes for Study

When studying for a test, some students do not know how much emphasis to place on topics presented during a chapter. As a result, they may overstudy small details and insufficiently review major blocks of information. Good notes should reflect the emphasis a teacher places on material, as should a test. During review sessions, show students how to apportion their study time for different topics based on the emphasis given in class and reflected in their notes. When handing back a quiz or test, show students where the information they should have studied can be found in their notes.

Suggestion 5: Apply Organizational Skills

Encourage application of organizational skills to improve note-taking ability, including:

1. Bringing proper materials to be prepared to take notes

2. Keeping notes organized (i.e., dating pages, maintaining a different notebook for each class, organizing notes at the end of each day and week)

3. Using a calendar to plan time for revising and studying notes

4. Reading assigned material prior to listening to a lecture

Summary

Note taking describes a range of techniques that enable students to study information later. Taking notes encourages students to be more active learners by processing information and writing it in their own words.

Notes from written sources should be used to introduce note-taking skills. A progression should be followed which begins with lists, then short, structured material, and finally multi-paragraph, less-structured material. The two-column method of note taking, in which main ideas are listed on the left side of a note page and details on the right, is the best approach for introducing and strengthening note-taking skills.

Four subskills should be taught to improve note taking:

1. Abbreviating

2. Employing word economy

3. Using visual markers

4. Editing notes

Note taking from lectures and other nonwritten material should be taught after the student can confidently take notes from written sources. The two-column method can also be used for notes from these sources. Taking notes from an interview is a good way to introduce this type of note taking, because the student maintains control of the content and rate at which it is presented.

Selective note taking is an advanced skill, which entails reviewing a source to find specific information that supports a particular topic. This skill is useful for completing research reports. Skeleton notes of major, minor, and paragraph ideas are also an advanced form of note taking that is useful for taking notes from lengthy reading sources such as textbooks.

Chapter 5 ◆ Summarizing

Summarizing helps students identify and organize the essence of the material they must learn. Sometimes there is so much information that students get lost in the details; a summary enables them to see the greater picture. By searching for relevant main ideas and creating a shortened version of the original material, students become active readers and listeners. Reprocessing the information to produce a summary provides practice for expressing that information in the student's own words.

Teaching Summarizing Skills

Introduce summarizing by discussing how it is a useful skill outside the classroom. Our society places a premium on being able to get to the point, and there are many examples in daily work, family, and social situations that call for summarizing. Business people want to know the "bottom line," doctors must summarize a condition and course of treatment, attorneys can win cases with good summaries, and newscasters summarize stories. We appreciate the friend who gives us a good summary of the movie we are thinking of seeing, but we might not ask their opinion again if all they give us is a lot of details that are out of sequence.

Just about anything in school can be summarized: a class lecture, an essay, a news article, a movie or filmstrip, a historic event, a scientific process, a short story, or even a varsity basketball game. As students develop summarizing skills, have them produce written and oral summaries from each of these sources. Keep in mind that the task of summarizing is not easy for students to learn. They need micro-united steps to follow, continuous practice with each step, and consistent feedback and monitoring. Provide significant practice to help them automatize the skill.

Using Two-Column Notes

Begin teaching summarizing skills by using two-column notes as a basis for creating a simple summary. The main ideas on the left side of the note-taking page form a basic outline; the student turns these main idea phrases into sentences to write a summary. Example 5A includes notes taken from the article "Juvenile Juries" in Chapter 4. The main ideas from the left column and a few supporting details are turned into sentences to create a concise summary of the original article.

Use two-column notes from previous lessons to practice this skill, and when students take new notes, ask them to use these notes to write a summary. With high school students, requiring summaries from lecture notes will develop good habits for actively reviewing these notes.

While "Juvenile Juries" lends itself easily to summarizing with its brevity and clear main ideas, most summaries are more challenging and require a great deal of monitoring by the teacher. First of all, be specific about what you expect in a summary by providing a general guideline for students to follow, such as example 5B.

Depending on the level of the students, any one of the steps in example 5B may pose problems. Distinguishing main ideas from details is never an easy task. Students will need continual practice. Problems may also arise when it comes to grouping the main ideas into logical categories and writing them into a unified paragraph. First, students must learn that the order of main ideas is flexible once they are taken out of the text; two main ideas may be combined or the last main idea may become the first sentence of the summary. There is no set formula for determining the order of main ideas, so the best way to teach it is through modeling and class discussion.

A good summary requires the application of basic writing techniques. Students need reminders to begin paragraphs with topic sentences and to write in complete sentences. Without the cushion of explanatory details, main ideas must be related by an occasional transitional word.

Example 5A

Two-Column Notes from "Juvenile Juries"

Main Ideas	Details
1. juvenile offenders sentenced by juvenile jurors in Denver	student jurors volunteer
	only sentence offenders who admit guilt and sign contract with district attorney
	sentences — community service, strict curfews, school attendance, job, pay back for theft
2. juvenile jurors popular	better than judge, more understanding
3. juries give sensitive, imaginative, and effective judgement	join athletic team
	letter of apology
4. reasons for jury program success	hearing soon after arrest
	believe young people responsible for actions
	good follow-up remembering birthdays and holidays
	only 1 in 55 sentenced twice

Summary of "Juvenile Juries"

Juvenile offenders in Denver are being sentenced by juvenile jurors. The juvenile jurors are popular because offenders feel they are more understanding than a judge. The juries have given sensitive, imaginative, and effective judgments. The main reasons for the program's success are that the kids receive a hearing soon after the arrest and the district attorney's office has a good follow-up.

Example 5B

Student Sheet: How to Write a Summary

1. Read the material and distinguish the main ideas from the details.

2. List the main ideas in phrase form.

3. Group the main ideas into logical categories—the order in which you read the main ideas is not always the best order for writing a summary.

4. Combine the main idea phrases into a paragraph using transitional words—include a topic sentence.

5. Proofread a first draft for punctuation, spelling, and unity.

6. Make a final copy with neat handwriting.

Using a Variety of Materials

Whether or not two-column notes are used to introduce summarizing, be sure that the material used at first is structured and not so long that students are overwhelmed. As they develop better summarizing skills, use less structured material that is longer and more complex. Summaries from scientific material may be harder to write than summaries from social studies material, or vice versa, so be sure to have students practice summarizing material from different subject areas. Here are some suggestions for integrating summarizing skills into classroom work:

1. When reviewing material in class, ask questions that require students to summarize information.

2. Give students prepared summaries as models of what was covered in class during the week.

3. At the end of a lecture, or to review an assigned reading, have the class develop a summary that you write on the board through discussion.

4. Ask students to present oral summaries as reviews of assigned readings or previous lectures.

Reading or listening to student summaries is one way of knowing which students really understand the content you are teaching and who may still need more instruction.

Any of the lessons suggested in Chapters 3 and 4 (Main Idea and Note Taking) can be expanded to include formulating summaries from the main ideas. Skeleton notes from textbooks can be used as outlines for writing section and chapter summaries. As noted earlier, creating a summary promotes practice with expressing important information and concepts in the student's own words. Writing summaries on a daily and weekly basis will ensure consistent and steady review of material, and the summaries can be used later as overviews when studying for a test.

When using a variety of materials, provide students with specific summary guidelines that clarify what should be included in each summary. Teachers can have students fill in answers to a question or outline sheet so that they will see more clearly how the task can be micro-united. Example 5C is a guideline that a student can use to write an opinion summary from a current events article.

Example 5C

Student Guideline for an Opinion Summary

1. State the main idea of the article; use this as your opening sentence. _____
   _____
   _____
   _____

2. What is your opinion concerning this main idea? Use a complete sentence. _____
   _____
   _____

3. Make at least two different points that would support why you think the way you do. Give evidence from the article if possible. _____
   _____
   _____
   _____
   _____
   _____

4. Write a concluding sentence that restates your position.
   _____
   _____
   _____
   _____

5. Combine your answers above into a paragraph to create your opinion summary of the article.

As suggested in Chapter 3, literary sources provide a good opportunity for practicing main-idea skills as well as summarizing skills. Once students have learned how to formulate a list of main plot events from a story, they can use these lists to write plot summaries. Main ideas from the story "The Christmas I'll Never Forget" in Chapter 3 have been turned into a summary in example 5D.

Writing summaries from literary sources is not only a good way to practice summarizing skills; it is also an organized way to remember important events and characters in long stories.

Example 5D

Main Idea List: "The Christmas I'll Never Forget"

1. On the way to meet his wife and family, John Horan's plane ices over and tilts to one side.
2. Horan parachutes out of the plane which enables it to land safely.
3. Horan finds a cabin, lives on cocoa until it is gone.
4. He decides to walk, tries to make snowshoes.
5. Shingles fail, but refrigerator shelves work and he walks until he finds two men who rescue him.
6. Snowshoes from refrigerator shelves were the best Christmas present he ever received.

Summary

John M. Horan keeps a pair of refrigerator shelves and puts them under his tree every Christmas because they saved his life. Years ago, when he was flying over Washington state on the way to meet his family at Christmas time, the plane he was in had trouble and he parachuted out. He fell safely to earth and walked in search of a highway. He came to a cabin and waited there for help until the cocoa, his only source of food ran out. He needed snowshoes to walk for help, so he made them out of refrigerator shelves. With the help of the shelves, he walked until he was rescued by hunters. He considers those shelves which saved his life his best Christmas present ever.

Paraphrasing

Paraphasing means expressing information in one's own words. In order to create effective summaries, prepare for tests, write good essay test answers, and avoid plagiarism when writing reports, students must develop good paraphrasing skills.

Students often confuse paraphrasing with summarizing, and it is important to differentiate between the two. A summary is a shortened version of the original which contains only the main ideas. A paraphrase is a restatement of a passage or sentence in one's own words without changing the meaning. Paraphrasing is different from summarizing in that the length does not change, and details are included.

Paraphrasing is helpful in three situations:

1. Rewriting lengthy, complex sentences into several, simpler sentences

2. Replacing difficult vocabulary words or phrases

3. Explaining concepts in the student's own words

Many students have difficulty comprehending and remembering the information found in compound or complex sentences. It may also be difficult to remember information if a sentence contains several difficult vocabulary words. Students must analyze the meaning as they translate these sentences, step by step, into easier terms. They are also much more likely to comprehend and remember a difficult concept if they have explained and rewritten it in their own words.

Several lessons can be presented to teach paraphrasing in these three situations. Pull out difficult sentences from class reading material and write them out on the board in logical sections. Ask students to give suggestions for how each section could be rewritten into a simple sentence. When working with sentences that contain difficult vocabulary, have students substitute familiar synonyms in place of the unfamiliar vocabulary.

Show students how to paraphrase concepts by starting with simple examples of figurative language and asking them to explain the meaning of the phrase in their own words. For example:

♦ Don't count your chickens before they hatch

♦ We'll cross that bridge when we come to it

♦ Six of one, half dozen of the other

Pictures or political cartoons with implied messages are also fun to use as a way of showing students how to paraphrase concepts.

Entire paragraphs in textbooks often have to be translated into simpler language to paraphrase the idea or concept presented. Encourage students to ask you to paraphrase particularly difficult passages in class. At the advanced level, opportunites to practice paraphrasing major theories and complex ideas can be found in all subjects, including science, sociology, political science, psychology, and economics.

Summary

There are many everyday examples of the value of summarizing. In school, summarizing is an important skill because it enables students to focus on the most important information. Students can improve their retention of material by expressing the information in their own words.

The list of main ideas on the left side of two-column notes can be used as the basis for a simple summary. Students can learn and practice summarizing skills by beginning with structured, simple material and progressing to lengthy, more complex material. Summarizing skills should be developed by using material from a variety of subjects or content areas. Writing summaries from literary sources, such as short stories, is a good way to practice summarizing skills, as well as a way to improve retention of the events and characters.

Paraphrasing something in one's own words should be taught as part of summarizing skills. Lengthy, complex sentences or passages containing difficult vocabulary can be paraphrased so students can more easily comprehend and remember the information. Abstract concepts or complex ideas presented in textbooks can also be explained in the student's own words for improved comprehension.

Creating summaries of notes, assigned readings, and class lectures on a consistent basis will develop good review skills and provide a useful tool for studying information at a later date.

Part III

Advanced Skills

Chapter 6 ◆ Textbook Skills

Students who try to study from texts often make statements like, "I read it three times, but I still failed the test!" Many students who are not taught textbook skills will remain passive, ineffective readers and may eventually give up trying to learn from their textbooks because the process is too difficult and frustrating. Using a textbook is an advanced study skill that incorporates the basic study skills presented in Part I of this guide.

Teaching Textbook Skills

This chapter micro-units textbook skills and groups them into the following categories:

1. Identifying and using parts of a textbook

2. Previewing before reading

3. Organizing and learning information while reading

4. Reviewing and expressing information after reading

Identifying and Using Parts of a Textbook

Some students never learn how to use the basic parts of a textbook, such as the table of contents or index, as helpful tools for reading. Ideally, parts of a textbook should be reviewed by teachers beginning in the early grades when texts are introduced. However, instruction and emphasis on the use of all parts of a textbook should continue through upper grades as new, more advanced textbooks are introduced.

Set aside time at the beginning of the year for "getting to know your textbook" and examine the different parts of a textbook with your class. Whenever the text is used in class or a reading is assigned, point out how parts of the textbook can be used. For example:

◆ Encourage a student who loses his place to use the table of contents or index to determine where he should be.

◆ As new words appear in the text, have students refer to the glossary for definitions.

◆ When a new chapter or unit is introduced, have students examine the table of contents to see how the information is organized within the chapter.

◆ Examine reading aids such as graphs, pictures, or end-of-chapter guides and summaries when introducing a new chapter.

Referring to the different parts of a textbook on a consistent basis will help students feel comfortable about using the many helpful study aids incorporated in textbooks. The following textbook parts should be reviewed in class as the first step to teaching good textbook skills.

Title Page

◆ What is the title and what does it tell the reader about the main idea of the book?

◆ Who is the author?

◆ Is there more than one author?

◆ What significance might this information have for a reader?

◆ What does the copyright date tell us about how current the information in the book is?

Remind students that checking to see when a book was written and who the author is is helpful when selecting books to use for research.

Preface and Introduction to the Book

Encourage students to ask these questions after reading any introductory sections to help prepare for readings:

◆ What information do these give about the organization of the textbook?

◆ What are the main themes in the book and what is the author trying to accomplish in the chapters?

♦ Is there a particular bias on the author's part that the reader should be aware of?

Table of Contents

Learning how to use the table of contents is necessary for the student to understand a textbook as a whole. A review of the table of contents will reveal how information throughout the textbook is organized.

♦ How many chapters are there?

♦ Are the chapters grouped into larger main-idea units?

♦ What are the relationships between topics in chapters?

♦ How is each chapter organized?

♦ Are headings and subheadings used?

Practice using the table of contents to locate specific topics. Show students how a quick review of the table of contents can reveal major topics and provide valuable information on how to read the chapter by sections.

Visual Aids

If pictures, graphs, charts and other graphics are included in the textbook, encourage students to use them as they read. Take time in class to read the captions beneath pictures and have students find the section in the text that refers to the picture. Do not assume that students know how to read a graph, chart, or map. Provide practice exercises using these visual aids so students do not skip over them when they read.

Study Aids

Most textbooks offer study aids, usually found at the end of each chapter. Students frequently ignore chapter summaries, vocabulary and main-idea study lists, and chapter questions. Insist that they review these study aids before they begin to read. Once they develop the habit of using them, they will realize how helpful they can be. Review the questions or chapter summaries in class before an assigned reading to prepare students for what they will find in the chapter. Point out how chapters are organized throughout the book.

♦ Are headings and subheadings highlighted in some way (boldface print, larger letters, etc.)?

♦ Are new vocabulary words italicized or in boldface?

♦ Are margin notes provided, or are key points highlighted in some way?

Index

Provide practice assignments for finding topics and information in an index. Point out to students that they can make a topic more general or specific to help find information in the index. During class, students can work together in teams to find the pages where information on a selected topic can be found.

Examining and using the parts of a textbook in class shows students how these parts will aid in reading and studying. Take some instructional time at the beginning of the year to review this information and refer to these parts of the book throughout the year.

Previewing Before Reading

Previewing a chapter enables students to read with purpose because they can anticipate ideas presented in a chapter. Previewing also helps build curiosity and interest by giving students the opportunity to think about the topic in relation to previously learned information or personal experiences before they read.

Surveying

The first step in previewing is to survey the chapter. The student should spend a few minutes getting a general feel for what the chapter is about and how it is organized. This includes

♦ Reading the title of the chapter to determine the over-all topic

♦ Looking at how the chapter is listed in the table of contents

♦ Noting how many pages there are and if they are divided into sections

♦ Reviewing any graphs, pictures and their captions, or other visual aids

Prereading

The next step is to preread the chapter. While prereading, students skim the material and read the introduction, titles and subtitles, words in italics or boldface print, margin notes or other notations, the conclusion, and any summaries or questions at the end of the chapter.

While prereading, students identify any new or difficult vocabulary words, especially if the textbook highlights these words in some special way. Definitions of these words should be determined before reading to improve comprehension of the material.

Developing Questions

The best way to develop a purpose for reading is to formulate questions that can be used to search for answers while reading. Many textbooks supply questions at the end of the chapter that students can copy out and refer to as they read. An excellent technique for generating useful questions is to turn the chapter headings and subheadings into questions. These heading questions will help students determine main ideas in the paragraphs.

Developing good questions is a skill that needs to be taught. Without some instruction in formulating useful questions, students will often generate simple who, where, and when questions that do little to help them read critically. Learning to frame what and why questions will help them think about ideas and concepts as they read. Encourage students to develop a variety of questions that will help them identify factual and literal material, as well as interpret and draw conclusions from concepts presented.

Taking Time in Class to Preview

Surveying, skimming, and questioning skills all must be learned; yet teachers often take for granted that students are able to perform these skills. Taking time in class to apply previewing skills will enable students to develop the habit of applying them independently whenever reading is assigned. Students usually want to do the minimum yet get the most from their school work; they may initially see previewing as a superfluous task that is not worth the time. It is only after students have tried it and can see how their comprehension and memory are improved that they will accept it as a useful, and in the long run, time-saving skill.

When introducing a new chapter, have students look the chapter up in the table of contents and preread the headings and subheadings aloud. Before a reading assignment, give students a list of vocabulary words and take time to have them locate the words in the passage and discuss the meanings. After giving them a few minutes to preread the introduction, conclusion or chapter summary, conduct a class discussion about what they think they might find in the reading. This is particularly helpful if they will be reading the chapter later at home.

Finally, show students how to develop good prereading questions by providing numerous examples. In the beginning of the year, hand out questions that you have formulated. As the year progresses, have students generate and critique each other's questions. Take advantage of opportunities to distinguish between good questions and those that are too specific or general to be of help during reading. Many of the questions developed during this previewing stage can later be used to anticipate and study for test questions. When you hand back a test or quiz, point out examples of the questions that were similar to those formulated during prereading.

A student sheet, such as example 6A, can be handed out to remind students how to preview before reading.

Organizing and Learning Information While Reading

To read critically and commit information to memory, students must become active readers. They must search for answers to questions, organize main ideas and important details, and paraphrase information while reading. The best way to do this is to divide a chapter and read it in sections of several paragraphs to a few pages long. As the student reads each section, the following skills should be applied:

Highlighting and Margin Notes

In Chapter 3, Recognizing and Formulating Main Ideas, the importance of determining main ideas in longer selections was emphasized. Highlighting and writing margin notes help students focus on main ideas and important supporting details. How do you teach highlighting? Most high school students, and even many college students, cannot highlight well; they either underline almost everything on the page or only a few facts. Provide models of good highlighting and take time in class to discuss and fine tune the process.

Have students identify topic sentences or parts of sentences that state the main ideas in each paragraph. They can highlight using a special highlighting marker. When main ideas must be inferred, students can formulate them in their own words and jot them down in the margins next to the text. If students have learned how to identify main ideas, locating and highlighting main ideas in a textbook should not be too difficult.

Practice this process in class. Have students take turns reading paragraphs out loud. Decide as a class which lines should be highlighted and where it would be helpful to write a margin note. Have them use their previewing questions as guides. Point out that even something as long as a textbook can be broken down into manageable sections with main ideas. This will make the task of learning from a chapter easier.

Example 6A

Student Sheet:
How to Preview a Textbook Chapter

Survey

1. Read the title to determine the topic of the chapter.
2. Look over the chapter in the table of contents to see how many sections it has and how they are organized.
3. See how many pages are in the chapter and each section, and look over any graphs or pictures.

Preread

4. Skim the chapter and read the introduction, headings and subheadings, words in italics, margin notes or other notations, and the conclusion to help anticipate what you will be reading.
5. Identify new vocabulary words. Find their definitions and mark them in the book or on a piece of paper to which you can refer as you read.
6. Turn headings and subheadings into questions. Be sure to include why and what questions that you can try to answer as you read.

Reflecting While Reading

Thinking about the ideas presented in a reading selection and expressing those ideas in one's own words moves the student into the realm of scholarship. As students become active readers and reflect on the material in their textbooks, they improve their critical thinking skills. Many students get excited about developing this learning ability. Reinforce the fact that they are using their own thought processes when they read critically by asking them their opinions about the points the author makes and by having them give critiques of the reading. Insist on specific examples from the reading to support their opinion and structure assignments to require them.

At the end of every reading section, the questions formulated during prereading should be reviewed and the information from the paragraphs used to formulate answers. Ask the following general questions:

◆ How does this relate to what I have already learned in class and through reading?

◆ How does this relate to what I have learned in other classes?

◆ How does this relate to my own experience?

Skeleton Notes

In Chapter 4, skeleton outlines of main topics and supporting main ideas were introduced as a way of helping students organize and learn information from lengthy sources such as textbooks. Taking skeleton notes on salient main ideas encourages students to reflect as they read and will also enable them to study the main points at a later date without having to reread the chapter. Use class time to begin note taking, and have students finish taking skeleton notes for homework.

The goal of reading in sections, highlighting, making margin notes, and creating skeleton notes is to have students be active, organized readers so they can better learn and remember the information presented. Talk about each of these steps with your students, provide time during class to apply them, and assign them for homework.

Reviewing and Expressing Information After Reading

Any review after reading should include having students express the information to be learned in their own words. Simply reading a passage does not commit material to memory. Even students who have organized and learned the information may not be able to express adequately their understanding in class or on a test if they have not practiced expressing it in their own words. Strategies for reading with a purpose (formulating and answering questions, highlighting, reflecting, note taking) will improve long-term memory and offer some opportunity for putting information into the students' own words. However, there are several additional tasks that can be done to improve study.

Summarizing

Using the suggestions presented in Chapter 5 for turning two-column notes into summaries, show students how this skill can be applied to textbook reading by using their skeleton outlines to create a chapter summary. If the chapter is long, several summaries can be written, one for each section of the chapter. In order to create a summary, students must narrow the information down to its major points and describe them in their own words.

Modeling is a useful principle for teaching students how to generate summaries. Hand out a summary to go along with a reading when it is first assigned. After students have read the passage, spend time in class discussing where each main idea in the summary originated in the passage. Next, have students write their own summaries, providing a sample for comparison. Students can share and critique each other's summaries to see if they are complete. As noted earlier, textbooks often have summaries at the end of the chapter. Use these for comparison as well.

Answering Questions

Prereading questions can be used later to review a chapter. Students should use these questions and add new ones to compile good review questions that might be found on a chapter test. Have students write out answers as if they were essay questions on a test so they can practice putting the information to be learned into their own words. Students may be surprised to find that some of the real test questions will be similar to their own. Having already written about the topic, they will feel more comfortable about answering these questions during the test.

Reviewing Within 24 Hours

Reviewing notes and study material within 24 hours significantly increases the effectiveness of the review and retention of the material. Within 24 hours is the optimum time to review because much of the information will be remembered, and subsequent review and reciting will build on previous knowledge. If students wait longer than 24 hours, they will essentially be starting over in learning the information. This also holds true for studying information from lectures. Therefore, encourage students to review their notes either the same evening or the next day. Teachers can help develop a habit for immediate review by providing class time for reviewing notes or assigning it for homework.

During these initial reviews, all the notes, study questions, summaries, teacher handouts and any other material that will be used to study later can be organized and stored in a safe place. This should be done on a daily and weekly basis (see Chapter 7, The Landmark Master Notebook System). The more thorough the initial review and the more organized the material, the easier and more effective studying for the test will be.

Summary

Good textbook skills are based on the application and combination of the skills presented in Part I of the Landmark Study Skills Guide: organization, main idea, note taking and summarizing. This chapter presents textbook skills in four stages:

1. **Identifying and Using Parts of a Textbook:** emphasizes the review and use of various textbook parts such as the table of contents and index.

2. **Previewing Before Reading:** covers the skills of surveying, prereading and developing questions before reading. Teachers are encouraged to provide time in class so students may learn to automatically preview before they read.

3. **Organizing and Learning Information While Reading:** stresses active reading by highlighting, writing margin notes, reflecting while reading, and taking notes. Critical reading skills often improve as students learn to be more active readers.

4. **Reviewing and Expressing Information After Reading:** creating summaries and writing out answers to study questions enables students to practice expressing what they have learned in their own words.

Reviewing summaries, questions and answers, and skeleton notes within 24 hours greatly improves both the value of review and long-term retention of reading material.

Following the steps in this chapter for effective textbook use will not be an easy task, especially for students who are not used to spending the time to micro-unit a reading assignment. Even in a special study-skills class, it would take a great deal of practice to master these textbook skills. Learning how to use a textbook should be seen as a continuous process that takes place over several grades and is refined as students pass through high school and college. Teachers at each level can contribute to this process by providing class time to apply textbook study skills and encouraging students to do so when they work independently.

Chapter 7 ◆ The Landmark Master Notebook System

The Landmark Master Notebook System is an ongoing system of organizing, studying, and mastering material. The system has three phases which can be taught one at a time. The students first learn to organize their time and materials, then to study, and finally to master information. This is a long-term process that can be spread out over many grades. The following chart suggests at what level students may reach independence with each phase of the skill.

	Phase I Organize	Phase II Study	Phase III Master
Upper Elementary	with help	introduce	introduce
Middle School or Junior High	with help	with help	introduce
High School	independent	with help	with help
College	independent	independent	independent

Phase I: Organizing

In phase one, students learn a system they can use to apply what they have learned about organizing their materials, their time, and their study space.

Setting Up the Notebooks

A *working notebook*, one of the most important organizational tools a student can have, provides the basis for organizing materials. This notebook, usually a three-ring notebook with an attached clip, includes supplies such as:

◆ A three-hole punch

◆ A zippered pencil case

- ◆ Wide-margin (or law-ruled) filler paper

- ◆ Section dividers

In addition to the working notebook, the master notebook system includes an *assignment plan book*, a *reserve notebook*, and a *reference notebook*. The students should also have a bookbag large enough to carry the master notebook and their other textbooks, as well as any other supplies they will need in their "portable office." Using this system, students can organize all of the materials they need for classes or for completing assignments.

Once the students have obtained all of the suggested components, you can begin to teach them how to use each part for organizing their materials.

Working Notebook

The working notebook, as the name suggests, is brought to each class and is the notebook in which notes are taken, handouts and completed tests filed, and so forth. Anything which might be required during a class period is kept in the working notebook. Any "live" notes (notes on material which has not been on a test yet) should stay in the working notebook so students can review and refer to the information in those notes while in class. Handouts given out in class can be immediately dated and placed in the rings of the notebook using the three-hole punch kept in the notebook.

Students can be taught to use the working notebook in class by taking time at the beginning of the year to set up the notebook and then providing time in class for students to organize, punch, and store papers whenever you give handouts. Some students may benefit from individual help in organizing at the beginning, or may need to be paired with another student who can assist them. It is important that they not only be able to organize their notes in their working notebook, but that they understand the reasons for setting up the notebook this way and maintaining it. If they know and can verbalize the rationale, they will be able to check their own progress and the effectiveness of this strategy and are more likely to use it in other classes and academic situations.

Reserve Notebook

The reserve notebook is used to store notes and papers that are not currently needed in class but that will be needed again for a cumulative exam, for a term paper, or for review in the next section of a sequential course. If students establish a place to store these papers, they will be less likely to lose or throw away materials which they will need later. The reserve notebook does not actually need to be a notebook, although a three-ring binder works fine. A drawer in a desk or a cardboard box will work just as well, as long as there is a way for papers to be separated by units or chapters. Manila file folders work very well for this purpose. Students should be taught to remove materials from their working notebook that are no longer current and to organize them into a packet by making a cover sheet for each set of papers that includes:

1. The dates covered by the material

2. A list of the contents by topic

3. A summary of the main points of the unit

The cover sheet in example 7A is a sample from an introductory biology unit.

Reference Notebook

The third notebook in the master notebook system is the reference notebook. This is another small three-ring binder, or a section of the working notebook, in which students store handouts given by their teachers containing information, directions, or examples that might be useful at a later time, even in another class. Students usually throw away these valuable guides because their immediate usefulness has expired and students do not know where to store them. If students keep them, they usually file them with class notes where they are difficult to locate. Students can be taught what to include in a reference notebook by your suggestions. Some items commonly filed in the reference notebook are:

♦ A personal spelling list

♦ Student sheets such as "how to answer an essay question"

♦ Samples of equations and how to solve them

♦ A list of transitional words and phrases used in writing

Example 7A

Sample Cover Sheet for Reserve Notebook

Biology

March 28 - April 5

Contents:

History of Biology

    Prescientific: explaining nature through gods or supernatural

        Egyptians: Ptolemy—knowledge of biology but prescientific explanations

Scientific era: reason, natural causes, observation

    Greeks: rationalism

        Hippocrates—father of biology

    Romans:

        Dioscorides—father of pharmacology

        Pliny—encyclopedia, collected knowledge

    Middle Ages: Islam added to Greek knowledge (e.g., algebra)

    Renaissance: dissection, primary observation

Summary:

Biology developed slowly over the history of mankind. In the prescientific era, people explained nature through gods or the supernatural. Although cultures such as the Egyptians had a knowledge of biology and the human body, they still explained things through the supernatural. The Greeks began the scientific era of rationalism, finding natural causes through observation. Hippocrates was the father of biology, the first to look for natural causes for disease. The Romans also contributed to the development of science. Dioscorides, the father of pharmacology, categorized plants and studied how they affected the body. Pliny also advanced the cause of science by collecting knowledge the Greeks had discovered. In the Middle Ages, the followers of Islam added the study of Algebra to the knowledge the Greeks had already developed. Biology and the scientific method developed even further in the Renaissance through methods of primary observation such as dissection. This laid the foundation for the scientific methods we use today.

- A sample of a completed assignment, such as a critical review of an outside reading selection

- Directions for completing assignments frequently given, such as a lab report

Any of the student sheets found throughout this guide can be given to students and kept in this reference notebook. Keeping them separate and accessible is the key to keeping them useful.

The use of both the reserve and reference notebooks is best taught by first providing supervised time in class to set them up and maintain them. Gradually shift to assigning them as out-of-class work that is checked in class, then to suggesting their use and telling students to find time to maintain them. In time, students will use them independently, without reminders, when they see the benefits of following the system. Emphasize their value by

- Including questions on tests about how to set up and use these notebooks

- Allowing students to use their reference or reserve notebooks during open note tests

Organizing Time and Study Space

In addition to organizing their materials, students need to learn to organize their time on three levels: long-range planning, short-range planning, and immediate planning. The best tool for long-range planning is a wall calendar or other large calendar on which the students can note any assignment due dates, test dates, other course requirements, and events in their personal life. While long-range planning organizes the student's time in terms of due dates and broad events, the short-range planning calendar is used for the specifics of what has to be done: recording and planning assignments and study activities. A planning tool that is especially effective for this is a teacher's plan book or similar weekly calendar book available in stationery stores. The final step in organizing time for students is to plan their immediate use of time: what they will do right now when they sit down to study. In addition to organizing their time, students need to set up and maintain an organized study space. Extensive suggestions for teaching students to organize their time and study space are given in Chapter 3, Organizational Skills.

By applying the systems described in this section and in Chapter 3 for organizing materials, time and study space, most students will find their academic work improves as their level of independence increases. The next phase of the master notebook system, the studying phase, allows them to go even further toward independently learning the information presented to them in classes and textbooks.

Phase II: Studying

In phase one, students learn systems for organizing their materials and time; in phase two, they are taught systems to use when studying the information they are learning in classes. Strategies for independently learning information from textbooks and lecture material, based on a two-column note-taking method, are suggested for this purpose.

The Master Notebook Study Strategy

The Master Notebook Study Strategy is adapted from a system of taking and learning lecture notes developed at Cornell University to increase greatly the efficiency and effectiveness of students' learning of lecture notes.[1] In this phase, the strategy consists of a three-step study process: record, reduce, and recite.

Record

The first step in the Study Strategy is to record notes in two-column form. During lectures, students should concentrate on recording only the details during the lecture, formulating the main ideas later. For lectures or notes from textbooks, they should skip a line between ideas, and leave spaces with question marks for information that is missed during the lecture. (See Chapter 4, Note-Taking Skills.)

Reduce

After the information is recorded, the next step is to reduce the notes to main ideas in the main-idea column, editing and revising them where necessary.

---

[1] Walter Pauk, *How to Study in College* (Boston: Houghton Mifflin, 1962).

Recite

Once accurately recorded, and then revised and reduced to main ideas, the notes are ideally set up for learning the information by reciting the notes. In this step, students cover the detail column of the notes, then turn the main ideas into questions and answer them.

Teaching Strategies

A natural place to introduce the Study Strategy to students is during a review session in class. If students already know how to take two-column notes, you can introduce this phase by modeling it in class.

First, after a lecture, demonstrate out loud and on the board how to reduce the notes to main ideas and recite them. After modeling the skill in this way, let the students practice independently by allowing time in class for students to reduce and refine their notes, and then having them recite to each other in pairs. When they are comfortable with this process, they can be assigned to do the same at home for homework. After a time of consistently assigning the recitation of notes for homework, and after you have had a chance to point out to them how following this procedure has improved class discussions, class work, test scores, or whatever improvement you have seen, move from assigning the recitation to suggesting that they continue to do it on their own, and that they try it in other classes. Periodically, as review, use the study system as a class activity to be sure they are still precise and thorough in their application of these skills.

Phase III: Mastering

Once students are routinely able to study their notes, they are ready to learn the Master Notebook Mastery Strategy. This phase has two steps: expressing and reviewing.

Expressing the Information in the Student's Own Words

The first step in the Mastery Strategy is for students to express the information from notes in their own words. Thinking about the notes and expressing those thoughts in some way provides not only a way of continually preparing for tests, but the opportunity for students to learn a subject so well that they can offer original thoughts or observations on it based on reflection. Using the blank, reverse side of a page of notes (the "mastery" page) as a work area, ask students to complete the following steps:

1. Write possible test questions based on the lecture and text readings from that day. Answer them in writing as completely as possible. Check your questions and answers with another student, and ask the teacher for clarification or assistance if you are confused or unsure about the information.

2. Draw diagrams, maps, or pictures to represent the information in a nonverbal way, if possible.

3. Prepare flash cards for memorizing details (definitions, formulas, names and dates, etc.) and quiz yourself throughout the week. Mark a card each time you miss the answer. When you have several marks, set the card aside for special attention. When you correctly identify a card several times, remove it from the pile — you have learned it! Learn the cards "backwards and forwards"; identify them from the front or from the back.

4. Invent acronyms or other mnemonic devices to remember facts or lists of information. (e.g., "HOMES" to remember the Great Lakes: Huron, Ontario, Michigan, Erie, and Superior).

5. Write a summary of the information that includes all the main points from each week. Stress finding a central theme that ties all the main points together, and use transitional words or phrases to show how ideas are related to one another.

6. Look for relationships and connections among ideas and write down the questions they raise. Ask connection questions, such as

   ♦ How does this relate to other things I have read or heard? (books, articles, handouts, discussions)

   ♦ How does this relate to other classes?

   ♦ How does this relate to my own experience? (things I have seen or things that have happened to me)

7. Then write down your comments and reactions, making a note of questions to bring up in class.

Reviewing the Information

The final step in the Mastery Strategy is a weekly review. One day a week should be set aside for each subject to review notes by reciting them again. For example, on Mondays, in addition to regular assignments in all subjects, time can be set aside for an English review. History is reviewed on Tuesday, science on Wednesday, and so forth. This keeps the information live, so that when the test comes, it does not have to be relearned.

During a weekly review session, ask students to do the following things:

1. Recite all of the notes in the working notebook from the beginning. Even though you will be adding more notes to review each week, each weekly review session will not take significantly longer. You will not have forgotten most of the notes from the last time you reviewed or from the initial learning.

2. Go through your notes and papers to determine what you can remove from your working notebook and put in your reserve notebook. Make a coversheet for the papers that includes the dates covered by the notes, a topical outline, and a summary, as explained in the section on the Reserve Notebook in this chapter.

3. Review any test questions, flash cards, acronyms, diagrams, etc. that you developed during the study phase. Refine and elaborate on your answers. Think again about the topics covered. Make a note of new ideas or questions to bring up in class.

Teaching Strategies

The Mastery Strategy can be introduced as part of a periodic review of material using the same techniques given for the Study Strategy on page 90. The skill-teaching cycle will be the same: teach students the steps to follow, then demonstrate them through class discussion. It is especially important to model the use of the mastery page in the notebook. After practicing the skill in class, assign students to do the same at home for homework. Review the Mastery Strategy as a class activity periodically so they can continue to refine their application of these skills. It is important that at each step of the process of introducing the skills you tell the students what they are doing and why they are doing it. This will encourage them to assume responsibility for monitoring the effectiveness of their study strategies as they apply them.

Summary

The three phases of the Master Notebook System are Organizing, Studying, and Mastering. The first phase, Organizing, involves developing a plan for effectively managing time, materials, and study space. The second phase, Studying, provides a systematic approach to learning independently textbook and lecture material by recording, reducing, and reciting information. The last phase, Mastery, involves expressing and reviewing material in order to deepen the student's understanding and ability to apply information.

The Master Notebook System is best introduced one phase at a time. Use the following skill-teaching cycle to teach each phase:

1. Model the skill

2. Use the skill with students in class

3. Have students use the skill independently

4. Review and spiral back periodically for greatest effectiveness

Students will not be able to use all three phases of this system independently as soon as they are taught them. Teaching the steps of the process one at a time, allowing time for students to develop independent habits, and monitoring student progress and application of skills will help ensure success.

Chapter 8 ◆ Test Preparation and Test-Taking Skills

Taking tests creates more anxiety for some students than any other school task. In order to do well on a test, a student must determine what to study, organize material, and express knowledge of that material in writing within a limited time period. All this must be done under the pressure of knowing that performance on any given test may significantly affect the grade for a course.

Teachers may assume that test performance is determined by how much time a student studies. However, test preparation and test taking involve complex skills that some students need to be taught in order to do well. Many students want to study but do not know how to do so effectively; others may have adequately studied the material but have a fearful, disorganized approach while completing a test and therefore do not do as well as they could. Instruction and practice with test skills can result in better test preparation, improved test performance, and reduced test anxiety.

Teaching Test Preparation

Test preparation begins on the first day of class and continues throughout a semester. If students apply textbook skills (Chapter 6) and keep master notebooks (Chapter 7), they will be constantly preparing for tests by reviewing and expressing in their own words the information they must learn from lectures, reading assignments, and class discussions. Refining and reviewing notes, creating summaries, and formulating and answering study questions on a consistent basis will prevent the need to cram large amounts of information just before a test. Reviewing material within 24 hours after it is first presented significantly increases the effectiveness of that review. By waiting until the night before a test, the student is trying to relearn weeks of information all at once. The anxiety that last-minute studying creates may erode student confidence and performance during the test.

Class Review

A good way to demonstrate ongoing test preparation is through class review. Many teachers announce a test date and give a class review a day or so before the test. Although class time devoted to providing study guidelines, answering last-minute review questions, and reviewing test-taking skills is important, the Landmark Study Skills Program advocates class reviews on a more frequent basis.

Reducing and Reflecting on Notes

After students have taken notes from a lecture or textbook, demonstrate out loud and on the board how to reduce the notes to main ideas. Then, through discussion, reflect on the notes. At first, direct the discussion with leading questions. Soon, with encouragement, the students will be able to direct the discussion themselves. Let students practice independently by allowing time in class for students to reduce and refine their notes, and eventually assign them to do the same for homework. This same procedure should be followed for creating summaries and using study questions. As review, periodically practice this procedure in class to be sure students are still precise and thorough in their application of these study skills. This will not only ensure that they know the skill, but that they apply it on a consistent basis. It is important that at each step of the process you explain to students what they are doing and why they are doing it so that they develop an awareness of how they learn.

Class Review Activities

There are some special class review activities that can be done just before a test. Instead of covering everything at once, spend a little time each day in class reviewing portions of the material. This will set an example of how information for a test can be studied in sections. Provide activities that enable students to be active during these review sessions. For example, instead of telling students what they should know about a topic for the test, write the topic on the board and have students determine what they think they will need to know. When asking study questions, do not accept one-word answers; encourage students to expand their answers by asking additional questions.

Reviewing Corrected Tests

Sometimes the most useful review time is after the test has been graded and handed back. Provide class time to analyze questions and determine what should have been studied. Students can learn from their mistakes as they go back over their notes, summaries, and study questions to correct answers.

Identifying Topics to be Studied

Besides class review and ongoing application of study skills, there are several steps a student can follow to prepare a week or two before a test. They can begin by determining what topics will be covered on the test and organizing this information into a list of main ideas, usually based on the same units they have previously organized and reviewed while keeping a master notebook. This list enables the student to micro-unit the material and study it one section at a time.

After announcing a test date, work as a class to have students generate the main-idea list. Ask them to think about how much emphasis was placed on each topic as the unit was taught, and use that information as a guide to determine what the test will include. In some classes, this list may need to be provided for students until they become adept at formulating one themselves. Students can be grouped into pairs to determine the topics for the test, and eventually this task can be given as a homework assignment.

Determining What Kind of Questions Will be on The Test

There is a strong advantage to knowing what type of questions will be on the test. Will it be all objective and short-answer questions, an essay test, or a combination of both? Students may focus their study and prepare differently depending on the type of information they must know for these questions.

Objective test questions (true/false, multiple choice, matching, fill in the blank) usually require the student to recognize or recall factual information, details from the right columns of their notes, and vocabulary terms. Covering the detail columns of notes and using the main ideas to quiz for these details is a good way to study this type of information. As a class activity, have students go through their notes to pick out terms or important details to put on flash cards. Students can quiz each other using these cards or they can have someone at home help them.

Essay questions, on the other hand, usually test for main ideas and concepts and require answers that reflect critical thinking. Writing summaries and answering practice essay questions throughout the semester will prepare students for these test questions. Remind students that knowing the answer is sometimes not enough; they have to practice expressing the information in order to perform well on essay questions.

Beginning in the elementary grades, instruct students in the different types of test questions that may be encountered on a test. Some students do not know how to answer matching or true/false questions. Review ways to approach these questions so students can be judged on their knowledge of answers rather than their ability to comprehend the question or method of answering.

With essay questions, words such as compare, contrast, define, discuss, relate, illustrate, evaluate and review have subtle differences in meaning; a review of these terms will improve a student's ability to answer these questions. Two essay questions about the same topic can require very different answers depending on how the question is phrased. Many students answer essay questions by writing everything they know about the topic and lose points because they do not address the details of the question.

Planning Study Time

Chapter 2, Organizational Skills, stresses the importance of teaching students how to use calendars and other tools for budgeting their time. Use time-planning strategies to plan how topics from a study list can be reviewed before a test. Once a test date is announced, note it on the large classroom calendar recommended in Chapter 2. Have students mark the date in their personal calendars. As a class, determine how many days are left before the test and plan time each day for studying. Show students how to plan some weekend time for studying while at the same time being realistic about other recreational and personal time commitments.

After the class determines a plan for studying, remind students each night what they should cover and, if possible, assign this as part of their homework. This approach will model organized test preparation and eventually demonstrate that this is easier and more effective than spending hours the night before trying to review everything at once. Using a calendar to plan study time is extremely useful when several tests are scheduled for the same week or day from different classes. Without some help in how to devise a plan of attack for studying different subject areas, some students may over-study one subject and neglect others.

Forming Study Groups

Joining together in study groups during class or at home is an underused study technique that can be helpful. Sometimes teachers recommend that students study with their friends, but most students do not know how to organize an effective study group and need to be shown a format that will make the time productive.

Study groups can include three or four students, although two students can be effective study partners. The group should begin to meet as soon as the test is announced. During the first meeting, students can organize what topics the group will cover. If each student in a group of four prepares ten good study questions, the group will have forty to use for review. Students can ask each other questions and give thorough answers in complete sentences. The student asking the question should have a written answer that can be used to fill in any information the other students may have missed.

Participation in this type of study process provides several modalities for reviewing information. In addition to reading and writing in preparation for the study group, the students also have a chance to listen to the answers given by others and then talk about them.

As a way of modeling this interaction, study groups can be formed by the teacher and meet during class time. Have groups create possible test questions and answer them. Include on the actual test some of the questions the students prepared.

The student sheet in example 8A reviews the steps for preparing for a test and can be passed out to students to keep in their reference notebooks.

Example 8A

Student Sheet:
How to Prepare for a Test

Throughout the Semester

1. Review and revise notes from lectures within 24 hours.
2. Highlight, take notes, and review all assigned readings.
3. Write summaries and answer study questions weekly from each unit of material.
4. Organize notes, handouts, summaries, etc., into your master notebook.

A Week or Two Before the Test

1. Form a course outline of all the main topics that should be studied.
2. Use a calendar to plan your study time; study the information in sections, and spread it out over several days.
3. Form a study group and meet at least three times.
4. Prepare for essay questions by predicting questions and writing out answers.
5. Prepare for objective questions by making flash cards.

Teaching Test-Taking Skills

Students' success on tests should be based on how well they have learned the material. However, a student who has not learned test-taking strategies may lose points on a test despite having a good knowledge of the material. Instruction on how to begin a test, how to answer different types of test questions, and how to answer essay questions will result in test grades that are a more accurate reflection of what the students have learned.

How to Approach a Test

When students receive a test, there are several things they should do before answering questions. First, they should skim the test from beginning to end to determine what kind of questions it includes and how they are grouped. They should note the scoring. Are some questions worth more points than others? How much of the score is based on essay answers? If students do not plan how they will proceed through the test, they may spend too much time on the first questions (which may not be worth many points) and not have enough time for essay questions at the end.

Show students how to develop a plan for how much time to spend on each section of a timed test. This plan should be based on how much questions are worth and how time consuming certain questions can be. Simply suggesting that students plan wisely is not enough. If they have not practiced this skill in class, many will simply fall back on old habits during the test. Mock test formats can be used in class to practice this timing skill (example 8B).

Example 8B

Test-Taking Strategy

You have one hour to finish a test. The test contains the following types of questions:

— 10 true/false questions worth 2 points each.

— 10 matching questions worth 2 points each.

— 4 fill-in-the-blank questions worth 5 points each.

— 2 essay questions worth 20 points each.

You should give yourself the following time to complete these portions of the test:

1. To skim the test _____
2. True/False _____
3. Matching _____
4. Fill-in _____
5. First essay question _____
6. Second essay question _____
7. Extra time to review answers and proofread _____

Show students how to go through questions and complete the ones that they can answer in a reasonable amount of time. If they do not know an answer, they can circle the question and not waste time trying to figure it out. If there is time at the end of test, they can go back and try to answer these questions. They should be sure not to forget to circle unanswered questions or they may have trouble finding them later.

Encourage students to develop the habit of reading directions carefully and underlining key words or important instructions. Points are often lost on tests because students have not followed directions. For example, sometimes true/false questions require students to rewrite the answer to make it true if they think the answer is false; if they do not read the directions carefully, they may neglect to do this. Sometimes misreading or leaving out a simple word can change how a question is answered. A multiple-choice question may ask a student to choose the best answer, but if this word is not noted, he may choose the first correct answer even though it is not the best.

The student sheet in example 8C is a guide for taking tests and can be given to students to keep in their reference notebooks.

Example 8C

Student Sheet: How to Take a Test

1. Skim over the test when it is handed out to determine what type of questions are on it and how much they are worth.

2. Plan how much time to spend on each section. Stick to the plan!

3. Answer the questions you know in each section and circle the ones you are unsure of. If there is time at the end of the test, go back and try the circled ones again. Do not waste time on answers you do not know.

4. Reread directions and underline key words. Be sure to follow the exact directions.

5. Leave time to review your answers at the end of the test.

Essay Questions

Many students answer essay test questions by reading the question once and then writing as much as they know about the topic (often in a steady, narrative stream). However, a more organized approach can be taught. Ask students to do the following:

1. **Analyze the Question:** Carefully read the question twice to determine what the teacher wants in the answer. Underline key words and divide the question into sections if it has several parts.

2. **Organize the Answer Before Writing:** Use an informal outline or list of ideas on a scratch piece of paper or in the margin to list the essential points you want to include in the answer. These notes are useful because, once you begin writing, you can easily forget to include an important idea or the answer to a second part of the question. This informal outline can also be used to help sequence the ideas in your answer.

3. **Write in a Clear, Orderly Style:** Begin the answer by stating exactly what you intend to do in your answer. This usually involves restating the question in some way. Then, develop the ideas noted in your informal outline by turning each one into a structured paragraph that states the point and includes supporting details or examples. Try to provide evidence to back up any statements or positions you take. Refer to the question and informal outline several times to avoid straying from the topic. Some students have the mistaken notion that the more they write, the better their answer will be, when in fact, teachers usually give more credit to a shorter answer when it is written in organized, concise paragraphs.

4. **Proofread the Answer:** Take the time to reread the answer for basic composition errors (punctuation, capitalization, sentence structure) and to be sure you did not leave out part of the answer. Always write your answers in pencil so you can make changes!

These steps can be practiced in class answering sample essay questions so students can automatize the process. If they go into a test situation and can automatically apply these steps, not only will their performance improve, but some of the anxiety about completing essay tests may diminish.

Give students a guide such as example 8D to refer to when taking tests.

Example 8D

> ### Student Sheet:
> ### How to Answer an Essay Question
>
> 1. Read the question twice.
> 2. Underline key words. Note how many parts there are to the question.
> 3. In the margin or on a scratch piece of paper, jot down and categorize information that answers the question in an informal outline.
> 4. Restate the question in an introductory sentence; state how you intend to answer the question.
> 5. Write out the answers following your informal outline. Use paragraphs and be concise. Give examples and supporting evidence when possible.
> 6. Proofread for punctuation, capitalization, sentence structure and to be sure you answered the question completely.

Test Anxiety

Most students can get over test anxiety with help from their teachers and application of good study skills. Failure in previous test situations is one reason why students dread taking tests, and the anxiety they feel from this may cause them to do poorly on tests when they really know the information. As noted in Chapter 1, providing opportunities for success is an important teaching principle and test-taking situations provide a good opportunity to apply this principle.

Plan the first tests and quizzes of the year to be short, simple, and designed to build confidence. This will help students who have a fear of tests realize that they can be successful at least some of the time. Give some open-book tests in which students are allowed to use their notes and other prepared study guides during the test. Some teachers do not like to give open-book tests because they feel students will not study; however, these tests encourage students to maintain a good master notebook and emphasize the importance of keeping good notes and saving handouts.

Curb test anxiety by allowing students to use a prepared one-page study sheet during the test. This sheet helps students who are afraid they will "blank" during the test. In some situations, it might be beneficial to model a good study sheet by constructing one during class time. This approach will reinforce the benefit of preparing organized, complete study guides.

Test anxiety can also be reduced by giving simple tests and quizzes frequently so they become part of the class routine. The more often students have to deal with tests, the more comfortable they may become with them.

The best way to help students overcome test anxiety is to teach good test-taking skills so they feel they are prepared before a test. Just as a carpenter who goes out on a job without any tools knows he cannot do a good job, a student who approaches a test knowing he is not prepared will also feel he cannot do a good job. Given the correct study tools, the test can be done well.

Summary

Good test skills enable students to prepare adequately for a test and then complete the test confidently and efficiently.

Test preparation is an ongoing process which begins with class review and independent application of note-taking, summarizing, and question-answer skills. Keeping a master notebook (Chapter 7) is a good way to consistently prepare for tests. A week or two before a test, have students identify topics to be studied and organize them into a main idea list. They should ask what type of questions will be on the test (essay, true/false, etc.). Study time can be planned in steps and spread out over time so it is not all left until the night before the test. Study groups of two to four students are useful for review of information and practice with expressing the answer.

Have students begin a test by skimming the whole test to preview the questions and determine how much time should be devoted to each portion of the test. They should then be sure to read the directions carefully. These are the steps to follow when answering an essay question:

1. Analyze the question

2. Organize the answer into a short outline

3. Write in clear, organized paragraphs

4. Save time to proofread the answer

A micro-united, planned approach to studying for a test will go a long way to reduce test anxiety. Taking tests and quizzes on a frequent basis may also help alleviate test anxiety. Test taking and preparation can be introduced and practiced in class until students can apply these skills independently.

Chapter 9 ◆ Research and Report Writing

High school and college instructors are sometimes surprised when students who usually do well in their classes have difficulty completing good research reports. However, given the many steps involved in producing a research report, it is not surprising that students who have not received instruction in how to complete such a project might not be able to write a report to the best of their ability.

It is therefore important that teachers in skill classes as well as content classes introduce report writing skills as early as the fourth and fifth grades, and continue this instruction through high school. The following skills should be included in this instruction:

1. Selecting and narrowing topics

2. Using the library

3. Collecting data from several sources

4. Organizing large amounts of information and creating topical outlines

5. Constructing a bibliography and assembling footnoting information

6. Producing first and second drafts

This chapter reviews how the application of the study skills presented in this guide can improve a student's ability to write a report. It also includes general suggestions for teachers when assigning reports. For more detailed suggestions on how to teach research skills, it is recommended that you consult one of the many instructional books available on how to complete a research project. The titles and publishers of three such books are listed at the end of this chapter.

Applying Study Skills to Research and Report Writing

Students will produce better papers if they can apply well-developed organizational, note-taking, summarizing and textbook skills as follows:

Organizational Skills: Organizational skills are useful for dividing a research project into steps and using calendars to schedule time to complete these steps. Good organizational skills are also useful for keeping track of notecards and bibliography cards when writing a paper.

Main-Idea and Note-Taking Skills: The ability to distinguish between main ideas and details and to apply good note-taking skills enables students to gather relevant information from sources. Note-taking skills also enable students to group information on note cards into main ideas that can be used to create a topical outline before writing a first draft.

Summarizing Skills: Summarizing and paraphrasing skills are useful for collecting information from sources. If students have learned how to write short, succinct summaries of reading material, they will be better able to create note cards from lengthy passages in books. Summarizing will also help them write the information they have collected into a first draft.

Textbook Skills: Learning how to use different parts of a textbook (table of contents, index, etc.) helps students locate relevant information in sources. Previewing and skimming skills allow students to quickly review sources to determine if material is useful without having to read in detail. Finally, highlighting, creating skeleton outlines, and reading notes enable students to efficiently and accurately collect information from sources.

Assigning Research and Report Projects

Teachers should give structure to a report assignment by providing specific directions and breaking the project down into a series of assignments.

Micro-Unit the Project

A completed research paper is the product of a series of steps that are completed one at a time. Emphasize this micro-united approach to completing a paper by handing out a list of steps that students should follow (example 9A), and monitor their completion of each step.

Example 9A

Student Sheet:
How to Prepare a Research Report

1. Choose and narrow a topic.

2. Read an encyclopedia entry or short article to familiarize yourself with the topic. This will help narrow the topic.

3. Brainstorm key words to look up when you begin to research your topic. Think about subtopics and words that may not already be in the title.

4. Formulate questions to help guide your search for information and organize this information.

5. Begin a topical outline.

6. Locate your sources: use the card catalogue, guides to periodical literature, encyclopedias and other references, primary resources, and audio-visual materials available on your topic. Do not limit your sources to books.

7. Collect information

    — Preread and skim for what is relevant

    — Discard irrelevant materials

    — Take notes on note cards

    — Paraphrase in your own words or note direct quotes with quotation marks

    — Mark page numbers and names of sources on each note card so you can properly footnote later

8. Make bibliography cards of all the sources you have used.

9. Construct a detailed outline before writing.

10. Write a first draft

    — Write information from your note cards and detailed outline into paragraphs with clear main ideas

    — Organize your paper into sections and use headings for these sections

    — Write an introduction and conclusion

    — Formulate your final title

    — Use footnotes to document where you found your information

11. Write the final draft: rewrite, delete, add, change the order, etc. to improve your paper. Proofread for consistent tense, spelling, capitalization, punctuation.

12. Construct a final bibliography from your bibliography cards.

Teach each step separately, making sure students understand the purpose of each step and its relationship to the other steps. Assign separate due dates for the different steps, such as

1. A narrowed topic

2. A topical outline

3. Note cards

4. A preliminary bibliography

5. The first draft

A grade can be given for each step of the project, as well as for the completed project. This will emphasize that the process for completing a good paper is just as important as the finished product. It will also provide structure for those students who do not plan well and who would otherwise try to do all the work at once.

Plan Enough Time to Complete the Project

When you assign a research paper, allow students enough time to adequately prepare for each step in the process and allow yourself enough time for skill instruction. For example, you might assume that students can choose an appropriate topic during one class session. However, teaching students the art of picking a good topic and narrowing it down so that it is manageable takes practice with several topics.

The goal for a research project should not be just the completion of a particular report, but for students to learn the process of report writing. Time should therefore be planned to analyze each step along the way. Have students hand in note cards, outlines and first drafts and provide class time to go over this material as the project progresses. It is much better for students to take a longer time completing one good report than to rush to complete two reports.

Provide Clear, Organized Directions

Provide clear directions and give structure to assignments. Hand out a calendar that notes due dates for various phases of the project and keep a copy on a bulletin board in class. Show students how to plan time for each step of the paper and be clear about what students are expected to do for each of these steps.

A good way to provide clear expectations for writing a report is to give models of what completed reports look like. Save topical outlines, note cards, first drafts and final papers from previous classes for this purpose. Include examples of work done well along with examples of poorly completed projects so students can compare and have a better idea of what they should and should not do for their papers.

Hand out a research packet when the project is first assigned that includes the following:

1. Cover sheet stating general requirements (length, number of sources, etc.)

2. Calendar with due dates

3. List of steps to follow that details each stage of the report

4. Requirements for and samples of note cards, footnotes and bibliography

5. Requirements and suggestions for first and final drafts

6. Summary of the grading criteria

This packet can be as detailed as you feel is necessary. Require students to bring it to class and refer to it every time you introduce a new step in the project. Even when students are capable of completing papers independently, hand out a packet to remind them of your expectations.

Summary

The key to writing a good research report is to break the project down into steps that are completed one at a time. Applying study skills (organizational, main idea, note-taking, summarizing, and textbook skills) will facilitate good report writing. When assigning a research report, teachers should:

1. Micro-unit the project

2. Plan enough time to complete the project

3. Provide clear, organized directions

Resources

Leahy, William. *Fundamentals of Research Papers*. St. Petersburg, Florida (Box 11120): Kenneth Publishing Co., 1983.

Yaggy, Elinor. *How to Write Your Term Paper, 4th edition*. New York, New York: Harper and Row, 1980.

Roth, Audrey J. *The Research Paper—Process, Form, and Content, 4th edition*. Belmont, California: Wadsworth Publishing Co., 1982.

Part IV

Parents and Students

Chapter 10 ◆ How to Be an Independent Learner

This chapter is written to show you, the student, how to do better in school by applying study skills independently. Parents, too, may wish to read this chapter to find out how to help students apply the skills in this guide.

Learning Principles

Chapter 1 reviews six principles that teachers can use to address the different learning styles of their students. Five of these principles can be described as learning principles that students can apply themselves when working independently. They are also prinicples that parents can use to help their children with school work.

Find Opportunities for Success

It is easier to work at something you are successful at than with something you have failed at before. Being successful on a homework assignment or on a quiz gives you the confidence to complete another assignment or test that might be more difficult for you. Sometimes school work is out of your control and you must do what the teacher has planned, but a lot of studying is in your control. Try to set up success situations for yourself.

The easiest way to plan for success is to be organized. Be ready when class starts by organizing your books and supplies ahead of time. If you do not have paper to take notes, or if you arrive late to class, you are setting yourself up to be unsuccessful. Follow the organizational suggestions later in this chapter to help you be successful when planning your studying and determining the most effective study strategies.

One way to create successful situations when doing homework is to start with a simple assignment that you know you can complete. This first successful assignment will give you the confidence you may need to tackle a tougher assignment.

When you find yourself in a new learning situation, such as the start of a new semester, do not overload yourself by taking on too much. It is better to be successful and receive good grades for a few courses than to struggle with many courses.

Finally, be sure to stay involved with interests besides school work in which you can be successful, such as sports, art, music, clubs, etc. If academics are tough for you, feeling successful about the other things in your life will make it easier to keep working at your studies.

Micro-Unit and Structure When You Study

Micro-uniting means breaking something down into smaller pieces or steps so that it is easier to study. All assignments and information presented in class can be structured this way and learned one step at a time. Sometimes a textbook chapter you must study, a composition you must write, or an important test you must take may seem too difficult a task, and you may not know where to begin. Try to analyze the task to determine what you might do to complete it one step at a time. Ask your teacher for help with breaking the task down into parts if you are having difficulty doing it yourself. When you micro-unit something, it is like drawing up a set of blueprints to get the job done.

There are several Student Sheets in this book that give ideas for ways students can micro-unit certain types of tasks:

How to Find the Main Idea (Chapter 3)

How to Take Two-Column Notes (Chapter 4)

How to Listen and Take Notes from a Lecture (Chapter 4)

How to Write a Summary (Chapter 5)

How to Preview a Textbook Chapter (Chapter 6)

How to Prepare for a Test (Chapter 8)

How to Take a Test (Chapter 8)

How to Answer an Essay Question (Chapter 8)

How to Prepare a Research Report (Chapter 9)

Make copies of these sheets, keep them in your notebook, and use them to help structure your assignments. (If you are following the Master Notebook System, put them in your reference section.) Planning and structuring work will take time and patience, but it helps you get the job done.

Use All Your Senses for Learning

One way to be sure you get the most out of a learning situation is to use as many senses as possible by listening, seeing, reading, writing or copying, and talking about the information you are trying to learn. Avoid situations where there is only one way to perceive the information. Some examples:

1. Ask the teacher to give you a copy of his or her notes or to put a list of ideas on the board when a lecture is given so you can see as well as hear the information.

2. When you have a reading assignment, stop at the end of each section and explain out loud to yourself what you have just read.

3. Copy information you must learn from a picture or chart so you are using more than just your visual skills to remember the data.

Remember, the more ways you work with information, the better your chances will be for understanding and remembering it.

Practice and Review

Sometimes we understand things the first time we hear or read about them, but if we do not review them, that understanding does not last. Get into the habit of practicing and reviewing new information soon after you have learned it, and continue to go back over it every couple of weeks.

Reviewing will ensure that you remember things over the long run and will make studying for tests much easier. As with learning to play a musical instrument or developing a new sport, the more you practice the better you will become. The term automatization, used in Chapter 1 for teachers, means practicing something until it becomes automatic. You will rarely forget something if you have practiced it to the point of automatization. The difficult aspect of practice and review is making sure you find the time to do it; that requires being organized and serious about wanting to be a good student.

The Master Notebook System, which is reviewed in Chapter 7 and later in this chapter, gives guidelines for applying study skills on a consistent basis and automatically reviewing.

Communicate

Throughout this guide, teachers are encouraged to discuss with students why, when, and how to apply study skills. Your school performance will improve if you are able to explain how you study and learn best. Your ability to remember information will also improve if you talk about that information in your own words. The following situations provide opportunities for you to discuss material you must learn:

1. Take advantage of opportunities the teacher offers to discuss and review material after school.

2. When the teacher asks if there are any questions about a lecture or the textbook, do not be afraid to ask for clarification.

3. Be an active participant during class discussions and do not be afraid to try and answer questions.

4. Find opportunities to discuss class notes or information from your textbook with other students in the class.

There are also opportunities outside the classroom to talk about what you are learning. Make arrangements with a member of your family or a classmate to help you study by regularly discussing what you are learning. Share your notes, summaries, and study questions with this person. Parents or older siblings sometimes want to help you study, but if you do not give them any information to use, or if you wait until the night before a test, they will not be much help. A study group is another way to be sure you have people with whom you can discuss your studies. Finally, you can always talk to yourself when no one else is available. Remind yourself of all the steps you are following as you study. Review information by asking yourself questions and answering them as completely as if you were explaining it to someone else.

Organizational Skills

Becoming an organized person is no simple task, but it can be done. As this guide emphasizes, teachers can do a lot in the classroom to help structure students and to teach them organizational skills. However, there are also some things you can do yourself to become a more organized, efficient student.

Organize Your Materials

You will need

1. An "organizational tool kit":

   ◆ bookbag (duffel bag, backpack, briefcase, etc.)

   ◆ three-ring notebook (a "working" notebook)

   ◆ paper, pens and pencils, other necessary supplies

2. A safe place to keep papers you will need later (a "reserve" notebook)

3. A place to keep directions and helpful student sheets (a "reference" notebook)

Helpful Hints

◆ Organize your materials for the next school day every night before you go to bed or every morning before you leave.

◆ Use a checklist of things you will need as a reminder.

◆ Refer to the chapter on organizational skills for other ideas.

Set Up an Effective Study Area

You will need

1. A consistent place just for studying

2. A table or desk roomy enough for all your supplies and clear of everything except what you will need for studying

3. Good lighting, minimal noise or other distractions, and a comfortable chair and work surface

Helpful Hints

◆ Study in the same place at the same time every day. Finding a place that you use only for studying will help you concentrate because it will not have other associations.

◆ Have all the supplies and materials you will need ready at hand.

Organize Your Time

You will need

1. A long-range calendar (wall calendar)

2. A short-range calendar (plan book or assignment book)

3. A daily calendar (list of things to do)

Helpful Hints

◆ Place the long-range calendar above your study space so you can refer to it easily while studying.

◆ Study at the same time every day. Use your short-range calendar to plan this. This will help you get started even on nights when you do not feel like doing homework.

◆ Use your plan book or assignment book all the time. Write down all the details of an assignment, and if you are not sure about something, ask the teacher before you leave class. **Do not rely on your memory alone**.

In Chapters 3 and 4, it was pointed out that most things can be categorized into main ideas and details. For example, the food in a supermarket is grouped into main ideas such as dairy, produce and meat. Almost everything you have to learn, including lecture and textbook information, can be grouped into main ideas and details. If there is a lot of information, sometimes main ideas can be grouped into larger main categories. Once you begin to group information in this way, it becomes easier to take notes, remember, and study what you must learn in school.

The best way to take main-idea and detail notes is to use a two-column format. Look over the student sheet entitled How to Take Two-Column Notes in Chapter 4 for details on how to set up your note page for this kind of note taking. This format produces organized notes that are easy to read and review. It is also useful for studying for tests because you can cover up the right side of your notes (the details) and use the main ideas as quiz questions. You can also do the opposite by covering up the left side of your notes and using just the details to quiz yourself on the main ideas.

Find the Main Idea in a Paragraph

1. Find the topic sentence.

2. If there is not a topic sentence, ask yourself:

   ♦ What is the topic of the paragraph?

   ♦ What does the author say about the topic?

Find the Main Idea in Readings

1. Start with one of your shorter reading assignments. Stop reading after every couple of paragraphs and ask yourself what the main idea of those paragraphs is. Put that in the left column (the main idea side) of your two-column notes.

2. Read the paragraphs again, and list the important details in the right column (the detail side) of your notes.

3. Ask your teacher to look over your notes to see if you are doing all right. Ask for help if necessary.

Find the Main Idea in Lectures

1. Use the two-column note format. Write down the details of the lecture as you listen. Skip lines if you think you are missing some information. Also skip a line every time the speaker seems to change topics.

2. After the lecture, fill in the main ideas in the left column. Fix up your notes, making them more complete and neat. This review will help you remember the information for the long term.

Textbook Skills

You can get the most from your textbook by applying a systematic approach when you use it. The first step before you begin to read is to familiarize yourself with the book and the selection you will read. This is called previewing and includes:

1. Surveying to get a general idea of what the chapter is about

2. Prereading the introduction, boldface headings, and special notes to help you anticipate what you will be reading

3. Developing questions to guide you as you read

Once you begin to read the chapter, there are several things you can do that will force you to become an active reader, which means carefully thinking about the information and putting it into your own words. You can be an active reader by

1. Underlining or highlighting parts of a paragraph that develop an important main idea

2. Making notes in the margins of ideas you think you should remember

3. Making a list of the main ideas on a separate piece of paper as you read

4. Writing a summary of these main ideas at the end of the chapter

Applying these steps will take time, especially at first when you are getting used to textbook skills. However, they are well worth the effort because they will ensure that you understand and remember the information you have read.

Finally, after you are finished reading, organize the notes, summaries and questions you wrote and review them on a regular basis. Regular review will make preparation for a test easier and more complete.

Using the Master Notebook System

The Master Notebook System is an organized, thorough way to get the most out of your textbook work, lectures, and assignments.

Organize, Study and Master Material

Read Chapter 7 to get a detailed description of how to use a master notebook, but here are the basic steps:

1. Set up and maintain a system for organizing your time and materials.

2. Systematically take notes on and review information from lectures and readings.

3. Each week, organize all assignments, handouts, notes, etc., and use them to make a list of the major topics covered that week. Formulate and answer study questions covering these topics. Keep these weekly study packets in order and review them every couple of weeks.

Preparing for Tests

Test preparation begins the first day of class and continues as you apply active reading skills throughout the semester and keep a master notebook to study information a little at a time. Before a test will be given, there are several steps you can take to ensure that you have adequately studied. The following steps summarize the ideas presented to teachers in Chapter 8.

Continual Preparation

Throughout the semester,

♦ Reduce and recite lecture notes after each class.

♦ Make study sheets, flash cards, outlines, summaries, charts, diagrams, and maps as you go along.

♦ Highlight, take notes, outline, or summarize textbook readings.

Special Preparation

Two weeks before the test, review

♦ Textbook readings and study guides you previously prepared

♦ Lecture notes

♦ Previous tests or quizzes

♦ Handouts from the teacher and homework assignments

How to review:

♦ Form a course outline; organize information from all of your sources into one, large outline (main ideas).

♦ Predict, outline, and answer essay questions.

♦ Quiz yourself for objective questions using flash cards, two-column notes, text highlighting, and study sheets.

♦ Budget your time so that all the information is reviewed without getting behind in your other classes.

♦ Study with a partner or study group.

♦ Never study by only rereading; you must do something with the information to learn it.

Summary

Students who are interested in improving school performance can apply the suggestions made in this chapter to improve their skills. Interested parents can also use this chapter to assist students in improving their study skills.

This chapter reviews the learning principles and study skills presented in the previous chapters for teachers. There are also a number of student sheets located in this book that would be useful for students to keep and refer to. They are listed on page 116 .